THE SONG OF ROLAND

THE SONG OF ROLAND

TRANSLATED INTO ENGLISH VERSE

BY

ARTHUR S. WAY, D.Lit.

AUTHOR OF TRANSLATIONS INTO ENGLISH VERSE OF HOMER'S ILIAD AND ODYSSEY,
THE TRAGEDIES OF AESCHYLUS, SOPHOCLES AND EURIPIDES,
THE GEORGICS OF VIRGIL, ETC.

Cambridge:
at the University Press
1913

CAMBRIDGE UNIVERSITY PRESS
Cambridge, New York, Melbourne, Madrid, Cape Town,
Singapore, São Paulo, Delhi, Mexico City

Cambridge University Press
The Edinburgh Building, Cambridge CB2 8RU, UK

Published in the United States of America by Cambridge University Press, New York

www.cambridge.org
Information on this title: www.cambridge.org/9781107667013

© Cambridge University Press 1913

First published 1913
First paperback edition 2013

A catalogue record for this publication is available from the British Library

ISBN 978-1-107-66701-3 Paperback

INTRODUCTION

AMONG the picturesque incidents of the Battle of Hastings, not the least so is that which preceded the onset, when—as Wace the Norman poet tells us in the Roman de Rou—

> "Taillefer, the minstrel-knight, bestrode
> A gallant steed, and swiftly rode
> Before the Duke, and sang the song
> Of Charlemagne, of Roland strong,
> Of Oliver, and those beside
> Brave knights at Roncevaux that died."

No more inspiring battle-chant was ever raised, having regard to the character, the traditions, and aspirations of the warriors who listened, and caught fire from his enthusiasm, as a thousand throats thundered forth the refrain " Aoi!" And to this day France has in all her literature no prouder heritage than this glorious war-hymn, which quivers all through with passionate loyalty, which throbs with loving patriotism, is fervid with adoring faith and utter trust in God, which is all aflame with that selfless heroism which takes no account of odds, nor holds life dear, nor dreads anything but dishonour.

It is a truly national epic. Such epics as those of Milton and Ariosto might have been written by a citizen of any country; but Homer's poems and the Song of Roland could only have been written by a Greek and a Frenchman respectively : hence they are national epics not only in their subject, but in their origin. Once more, the Chanson shares with Homer's works and the *Nibelungenlied* the distinction of being the only epics of natural growth, as distinguished from the manufactured epic, the production of a learned poet who has to re-create for himself an age into which he was not born. These are the sole examples of the spontaneous product. In each case the author (or authors) has idealized a less heroic foundation-story, and yet idealized it—not after the manner of Virgil or Tennyson—but only according to the standards of an age very close to, if not practically identical with, that of which he wrote.

In each case the poem, in the form in which it has come down to us, was the work of a poet who welded into a harmonious whole ruder materials—ballads, lays, or legends, which had their birth among the men of the very generation which played a part in the events immortalized in song. In the case of the *Iliad* we have no certain and definite knowledge of what these events were; but for the Song of Roland we are not in the dark at all. The chief heroes are historical personages, and their achievements have changed the history of Europe.

In the year 778, just when Offa of Mercia was in the height of his power, the Emperor Charlemagne was in Spain. His project for delivering the land from the yoke of the Saracens had been successful only as far as the Ebro, when tidings of a rising in Saxony, in the far east of his vast dominions, compelled him to return. Having stipulated for the payment by the Saracens of a huge sum in gold, and having received hostages, he led his army back over the Pyrenees. His main body threaded the passes in safety; but as the rear-guard, encumbered with baggage and treasure, wound slowly round the flanks of the Altobiscar mountain, an avalanche of broken rocks and trunks of trees, a rain of missiles, poured down upon them from a concealed foe, till, in the height of the panic which ensued, the Basque (or Gascon) highlanders burst forth from the black pine-forests which overhang the pass of Roncesvalles, swept down upon the thin, straggling, broken line, hurled it, soldiers, camp-followers, baggage-cattle, in hideous confusion to the gorges below. The chivalry of France fought desperately; but, encumbered as they were by the weight of their armour, separated from each other, hampered by non-combatants and beasts frenzied with terror, there could be but one ending. Among the slain the old chronicler Eginhard particularly mentions " Roland, prefect of the marches of Brittany." He adds, that the disaster was never avenged. The Basques vanished with their booty among their trackless mountain-fastnesses; Charlemagne's hands were full on his eastern borders for many years ; but, he adds, "this disaster clouded the king's heart with sorrow amidst all his successes."

Such is all that history tells us of the calamity of the 15th of August, 778. At first sight it seems inadequate material for a national epic—this surprise and massacre of the rear-guard of a retreating army. But there is a certain reticence in the old Latin chronicle which conveys the impression that the disaster is there minimized, as though policy forbade the telling of too much while the king lived. We can infer more from the eagerness with which popular legend took up the story. The bravery of those who perished, their previous exploits, their honour at Charlemagne's court, the pathos of their end, the mourning for their loss, all appealed strongly to the popular imagination. Revolts of the southern mountaineers were suppressed some thirty years later ; a great invasion of the Saracens was repulsed, and Catalonia and Arragon were definitely annexed : these events were connected in men's minds with the massacre, and soon appeared in legend as a swift vengeance which immediately followed. The jealousy and cupidity of highland tribes seemed unworthy and insufficient to account for so great a calamity ; so the legend transferred it to a treacherous attack on the part of a huge host of Saracens. Again—it is a characteristic national touch—it was deemed incredible that a French force should be defeated save by the treason of some one on their own side; so the final stroke was added, the invention of a traitor, to whom legend gave the name of Ganelon.

As the story, thus magnified, took hold of the public imagination, there were born of it, probably as early as the reign of Charlemagne himself, numerous popular songs and ballads. We find, from the writings of the historians of the time, that such ballads were sung through the length and breadth of the land ; they describe the country-folk chanting them, the women beating time with their hands; they tell how they were sung in farm and fair, in camp and court, and even at the vigils of the saints. These lays were by no means all confined to the subject of Roland, but, as time went on, the latter seems to have played the part of Aaron's rod to the rest, most of which were either merged in it, or forgotten. But there was as yet nothing epic about these chants or ballads. They were short, full of energy and melody, half narrative, half lyric, and served to keep alive the legend, till a poet arose who out of these ruder materials fashioned a great poem.

The Chanson de Roland, as we possess it, is not, however, the original epic. It was probably preceded by two others, no doubt shorter and less elaborate in style, and with less wealth of incident. One of these must have been that which Taillefer chanted before William's host at Hastings. Though they disappeared before the popularity of the final version, they left on it some curious traces of their individuality, and of the different periods at which each was composed; as, for instance, when we find the capital of France called in one place Laon, in another Aix-la-Chapelle, in another Paris.

The date of our version cannot possibly be earlier than the eleventh century, since it contains allusions to the capture of Jerusalem by the Saracens, which happened in A.D. 969, and to their murder of the Patriarch, which was perpetrated in A.D. 1012. Léon Gautier decides that it was certainly composed by a Norman poet, and probably by a Norman who had taken part in the conquest of England, or who had at least lived in England. Who the author was, we cannot tell. True, the last line of the poem is, "Here ends the *geste* which Turoldus *declinet*"; whence some have inferred that a certain Théroulde, Abbot of Peterborough, composed it. But, in the first place, it is not established that *geste* there means "poem," and not the "chronicle" on which the poem was founded, or that, if it does mean "poem," it refers to this Chanson, and not to an older one which formed the basis of it: secondly, the meaning of *declinet* is quite uncertain. It has been supposed to mean "completed"; but whether the reference is to the chronicler who completed the prose narrative to the authority of which the poet four times appeals, calling it a *geste*, or to the scribe who completed the copy which so ends, or to the *jongleur* who completed the recitation, or to the poet who completed the composition of it, no one can definitively pronounce.

The date of this final form of the epic, then, cannot be earlier than the eleventh century; and scholars mostly agree in placing it between the Norman Conquest (A.D. 1066) and the First Crusade (A.D. 1096). Whoever composed it, and wherever he lived, he can have had small reason to be dissatisfied with the reception of his work. It became at once to France what the *Iliad* was to Greece, the gospel of chivalry. The *jongleurs*, or bards, sang it from one end of the land to the other: it is in a wandering minstrel's pocket-copy that the only perfect manuscript of it has survived. It was for five hundred years quoted, as a solid historical document, on the faith of which its hero, already regarded as a martyr, narrowly escaped being canonized as a saint. The figure of Roland was tossed upon battle-flags, and shone upon the stained-glass windows of churches. Its glory inspired poets all Europe through, and Dante placed Roland high among the hero-saints of the Fifth Heaven in his " Paradiso." In the fourteenth and fifteenth centuries the glory of the poem seemed to have reached its highest point, when a misfortune befell it, which is almost unique in the history of literature.

With the coming-in of the sixteenth century the Renaissance dawned upon Europe, and men became aware of the treasures of poetry and eloquence enshrined in the works of classical antiquity. Beside the literary finish, the music, the magical charm of these, all works in their own tongues seemed coarse, harsh, contemptible: men were ashamed to be seen reading them. While the printers vied with each other in issuing editions of the Classics, no one troubled to copy, much less to print, poems in the vernacular, which were cast away to the lumber-room or to the flames. So France became so infatuated for the singers of Greece and Rome, that it consigned Roland to oblivion. Men were content, nay, complacent in a blind ingratitude to their glorious past; and this ingratitude was so unanimous, so complete in its results, that it lasted more than 300 years.

During all this time the name of Roland was preserved only among some poor peasants, who, on Sundays or Saints' eves, used to read the "Blue Library," a prose version of the old ballad-epics. As for men of culture, they knew not our hero even by reputation ; and it was an ignorance on which such autocrats of literary taste as Boileau and Voltaire did not scruple to pride themselves. We must take a leap of three centuries to alight in the midst of a France which falls in love anew with its national poetry. Chateaubriand, in his "Genius of Christianity," and Victor Hugo, in "Notre Dame de Paris," inflamed their generation with a passion for the Middle Ages.

Dim memories of the Chanson were revived ; but for the poem itself men looked around in vain, till, in 1837, Francisque Michel got on the track of a copy said to exist in the Bodleian Library, at Oxford. Thither he repaired, and day after day turned up at the Library, till he had copied the 4002 lines of the old text from the "Digby Manuscript," which is probably the only complete ancient copy of this epic left in all the world. It is very interesting, not only from its contents, but from its character. It is one of the little volumes actually used by the *jongleurs*, carried about with them in pocket or wallet in their journeys from castle to castle, and continually applied to in order to refresh the memory. It has been well thumbed, and the parchment bears the marks of many vicissitudes of travel. Unfortunately, it was not, when new, a blameless copy. The original scribe had here and there omitted a line, or part of a line : subsequent correctors, according to their lights, repaired omissions, improved the spelling, modernized archaic expressions, and squeezed in a few interlineations ; but, being not a whit more intelligent or well-informed than the original copyist, their improvements added little to its literary value, while detracting from its legibility. Fortunately, however, scholars have been able to supply conjecturally the defects of the Digby manuscript by the help of another, in itself greatly inferior and far more imperfect, which is preserved in St Mark's Library at Venice. There are also others, which are rather paraphrases than versions of the poem, from which the general sense of doubtful passages has been gathered. So near did the great epic of France come to extinction.

The versification of the Chanson has a character which has now practically disappeared from literature. The lines are not blank-verse, neither are they in rhyme, but in what is called *assonance*, that is, the last accented vowel-sound is the same, though the consonant-sound which follows need not be identical, as in rhymed verse. One of Father Prout's *jeux d'esprit* furnishes an example:

> "The Groves of *Blarney*,
> They are so *charming*
> All by the *margin*"—

That such a style of verse-composition could satisfy the hearer, is explained by the circumstance that in those days there were, in a popular audience, practically no *readers*, but only hearers. The wandering minstrel travelled through the land with his lute on his back and his manuscript in his wallet. On arriving at a town, dusty and travel-stained as he was, he took his stand in the market-square. At the first notes struck upon the strings, a crowd began to gather; and then and there the minstrel chanted some hundreds of lines to a delighted audience. Or he wended his way to the gate of the castle which frowned over the township. The heavy monotony of the long evenings made him a welcome guest. After supper, when "the tables were drawn, it was idlesse all," the castle household grouped themselves in the great hall; the lord and lady sat in their high-seats; and the minstrel gave an "epic séance" (as Gautier calls it), an evening with the heroes whose names were household words through Europe. Now we must bear in mind that his audience, none óf whom could read, knew words only by sound, and that criticism of the quality of verse in which the eye co-operates with the ear was wanting to them. Remembering also how usual it is for singers to touch very lightly, or to suppress altogether, the final consonant in a line, and bearing in mind that the poem was not recited, but declaimed in recitative, you will understand how the satisfaction was perfect to the ear of the mediaeval audience, who were only sensitive to rhythm and corresponding vowel-sounds.

The poem was divided up into stanzas, or *laisses*, of varying length, averaging about 15 lines each. All the lines of any given *laisse* were in assonance with each other. Each *laisse* ends with the refrain " *Aoi!* " which is probably of the same origin as our sailors' " Ahoy! " and so came over-sea with Rollo and his Norse vikings. It may have been designed to be caught up at regular intervals by the audience, as a vent for the emotions kindled within them by the recital.

When we pass on to consider literary character, as distinguished from technical form, we recognise that we are in the presence of a primitive epic. There is nothing of the consciously artistic in the style, nothing which suggests that the author thought less of *what* he had to say than of how to say it. Spontaneous and artless, it is the very opposite of the work of Dante or Milton. The poet is less burdened by misgivings as to the requirements of probability, of the necessities of time and space, of the limitations of human power, than is usual even in early epics. Heroes smite on, hour after hour, slaying, each of them, more foes than Samson : the blast of a horn is heard fifteen leagues away ; and an army returns from a two days' march apparently in an afternoon. Yet, for all that, the poem does not read like a fairy-tale, but as a veritable record of human achieve-ment, endurance, and loyal faith, idealized into the region of the super-human. The heroes themselves are no mere labelled fighting-machines : they are living men, each with a sufficiently individualized character. It is true that the characterization is not strong or elaborate ; it was not to be expected in a non-introspective age, when men were judged mainly by their deeds. As the heroes are truly human, so they are no whit ashamed of human weakness. They burst into tears of sympathy, of repentance, of sorrow. They tremble and sob with high-wrought feeling : they swoon when the effects of exhaustion are enhanced by strong emotion. The quick perceptions, the responsiveness to inspiring appeals, the adoring love of country, of the Frenchman, are already there.

In one respect the poem is unique among epic romances, in a feature which reminds us that it preceded the age of chivalry proper. It is marked by a total absence of love-passages or even allusions, save for a few lines in which we are told how Roland's betrothed falls dead on hearing of his death. But no warrior cries the name of his lady-love in the onset ; no vision of her fair face looks in through the mist of battle, no one remembers her in death, no tress of golden hair is stained with the blood which was shed all "for sweet France."

The religious atmosphere of the poem, the recognition of religion as an incentive to endeavour, as a consolation in death, is a real revelation of the spirit of the time. The Song of Roland is the first great popular poem which was written after the coming of our Lord; and the influence of Christianity on life, on thought, on men's motives and their aims, is most marked. God is in this poet's eyes a veritable Lord of Hosts, the Captain of the forces of Christianity against paganism. After reading the Chanson, we can better understand the enthusiasm with which Europe hailed the Crusades; for the spirit is already here, and we see how ripe men were for that great movement. Here are warriors who already battle for the Cross: Paradise is their assured reward; saints and angels descend to take away their souls. Here also we already find that peculiar ruthlessness, conscientiously cruel, towards foes of another creed, which attained its climax in the sixteenth century, but which was unknown in the world until men grafted some examples of Old Testament practice on the precepts of the New.

While in the execution of its author's conception, in inventiveness and dramatic grouping of incident, in delineation of character, in wealth of imagination, in poetic inspiration, in the magic of language, in literary finish, the Chanson is, as was inevitable, far inferior to the great epics of Greece and Italy, in one respect it may be claimed that it rises above them, that it stands on a higher plane. In its spirit, in the inspiring motive of its characters, it is the ideal of what a national epic should be. Patriotism, and patriotism hallowed by unwavering faith in God, is the key-note of the whole poem.

The *Iliad*, in its final analysis, is the glorification of selfishness. True, it is an heroic, a noble self that is idealized; the hero does well to be angry; he stands not only in defence of his own rights, but as the champion of other actual and threatened victims of tyranny: but in the course he takes he is not merely reckless of the calamities that will overwhelm those of his own race and country, he actually intends them; the death of thousands of innocent men is part of his scheme of self-vindication.   The note of patriotism, in fact, is absent.   It might even be argued that he does, in a magnificent, heroic, and open way, what Ganelon does in a mean, villainous, and underhand way.   But the Chanson is the paean of patriotism. "For God and my Country!" is the battle-cry that rings through it all; and this is never marred by one jarring note.   None murmur at the decision which has set them all in the face of death; no man flinches, and that because they will not shame "sweet France"; the last breath of the dying is spent in blessings on their fatherland, their king, and their friends; even in their condemnation of the traitor there is a tempered self-restraint, as though they recognized that the treason had been overruled for the glory of their country.

It is a curious circumstance that England stands almost alone among great nations in having no national epic.   France, Germany, Spain, Italy, Greece, and even Portugal, are all more or less richly endowed in this respect; but our own land has only a few stirring ballads, a few splendid outbursts in Shakespeare; and we may well envy France her possession of the "Song of Roland."

This version has been made from the great critical edition of E. Stengel, which contains 637 more lines than the Digby MS.   I have also included six lines at the end of *laisse* 31, and six at the beginning of *laisse* 39, taken in each case from Gautier's edition.   In two or three instances I have adopted a reading given in Stengel's notes instead of that in his text.

As a reproduction of the verse-structure of the original is practically impossible, and, were it possible, not to be desired, I have felt free to adopt a measure which seems to lend itself well to the interpretation of the spirit of such an epic, the same, in fact, as that employed in my version of the *Nibelungenlied*.

If any learned critic be inclined to censure me because I have not reproduced "the quaint simplicity, the artless *naïveté*" of the language of the original, I reply that I have purposely refrained from doing so, for two reasons. First, these features of the poem simply did not exist (in the sense in which they do for the modern reader) for those who listened to the minstrels as they chanted it. It was the highest type of heroic verse to them, as finished literature, we are justified in believing, as Walter Scott or Macaulay is to us. Familiar as they were with the life and action which it portrays, they heightened its descriptions with the colouring of their own experience, its passion with the fire of their own emotions. Hence a rendering which reproduces the verbal peculiarities of the old epic, however satisfying it might be to the pedant, would for the modern reader be beyond measure balder and less stirring than the old epic seemed to the men of the poet's age. Secondly, the translator who aims at conveying to the men of his own age something of the effect an epic produced on the ancient hearer whose "heart was stirred by it as with the sound of a trumpet," must needs introduce a certain glow of colouring, an occasional amplification in description, if he would set a situation as vividly before the former as it rose before the latter. And here I am consciously and emphatically at issue with Matthew Arnold, who avers that we cannot possibly know what effect was produced on the original hearers. When we know, from more than one allusion in the *Odyssey*, how, in the heroic age, a bard could hold his audience spell-bound—"Fain would they listen for ever, he sings each heart his thrall"; when we know that the rhapsodist could, even in the mid-noon of Greek literary culture, always gather an audience to listen with rapt attention to his recitation of Homer, that the poem so stirred even the reciter that he sometimes broke down in a passion of tears ; when we know that the minstrel who bore with him the Song of Roland was welcome in bower and hall, in market-place and on village green, that the chanting of a passage from it could kindle into flame the martial ardour of an army, we know more of the effect produced on the ancient hearers than any translator (as many have proved to their cost) can know of the impression destined to be made by his performance on any of those learned pundits whom Arnold recommends him to set before himself as his tribunal of final appeal.

A. S. W.

March, 1913.

THE SONG OF ROLAND

1

CHARLES, King of France, the mighty, the Nations' Overlord,
Through seven full years hath tarried in the land of Spain, hath warred,
Till even down to the sea's lip he hath conquered the mountain-land,
Till not one castle remaineth whose towers against him stand,
Till never a city nor rampart abideth not cast down,
Save Saragossa, the fortress throned on a mountain's crown,
Yet holden of King Marsila: our God doth he abhor;
He is servant unto Mahomet, and Apollo doth he adore:
But he shall not avert God's sentence thus, and the doom in store.

2

So there in Saragossa the King Marsila stayed;
And he passed on a day 'neath an olive, he rested under its shade.
On a slab of the sea-blue marble layeth him down the King,
And he smiteth his hands together for the griefs that inly sting:
There warriors twenty thousand, yea, more, stood round in a ring.
And he cried to his great war-captains, to his earls he bemoaned him thus:
"O ye my war-lords, hearken what evils encompass us!
Charles, Overlord of Nations, and goodly France's King,
Hath come into this our country for our discomfiting.
Ever he draweth nearer; I know how nigh is the fight;
Yet hosts have I none of prowess to shatter his iron might.
As beseemeth the wise and prudent, counsel me therefore ye,
And so from death redeem me, and save from infamy."
He spake; but of all those paynims was none that answered a word,
Till spake at the last Blancandrin, Castel-Valfunda's lord.

W. C. R.   1

3

Wise mid the wisest paynims Blancandrin was, and white
Was the hair whose silver ripples with his beard were mingled, a knight
Full knightly: for help of his liege-lord was he full of cunning sleight.
"King, be not dismayed," he answered, "but to Charles the haughty, the proud,
Send proffer of loyal service, and be utter friendship vowed.
Bears do thou send him, and lions, and hounds, as the gifts of a friend;
Let many a goodly war-steed and palfrey thy mission commend:
Seven hundred camels, and moulted falcons a thousand send.
Four hundred strong mules laden with gold and with silver prepare,
And money so much as fifty treasure-wains may bear,
Such glittering store of bezants of fine gold tried in the fire
That thereof he may fully render to his men of war their hire.
And say: 'O King, thou hast tarried so long in the land of Spain,
That well mayest thou turn backward to France and to Aix again.
At Saint Michael's Feast will I follow thee thither, thy proselyte,
And receive the faith of the Christians by holy baptismal rite;
And thy man will I be, with my substance and love to serve my chief,
And will hold all Spain, thy vassal, henceforth of thee in fief.'
Yea, hostages shalt thou send him, if this he require of my lord,
Be it ten, be it twenty, that credence be given so to thy word,
Yea, the sons of our noblest ladies; even thine thou shalt not spare:
Mine own son will I surrender to die, if it must be, there.
Rather it were to be chosen that the heads should fall of these,
Than that we should be stripped, a nation, of our lands and our seignories,
And that begging our bread we should wander in misery of want."
Then low the paynims murmured: "Yea, all this well may we grant."

4

Then spake yet again Blancandrin: "By this right hand that I lift,
By the beard that over my true heart light in the wind doth drift,
Thou shalt see yon host of the foemen break up in disarray,
And to France, to their own far country, shall yon Franks melt away.
So when to the homes that they long for they have scattered one and all,

Then Charles unto Aix shall betake him, to the Christians' temple-hall,
And there to his great Saint Michael shall he hold high festival.
It shall come, the day ye appointed, from noon unto night shall it wane;
But never a word of our coming nor tidings of us shall he gain.
O yea, yon King is haughty, and cruel his wrath as the grave;
He shall hew the heads from the shoulders of the hostages we gave:
Howbeit, were this not better, that they laid their lives down there,
Than that all we lose our country, our Spain the dear and fair,
And that we should endure tribulation and miseries worse than death?"
And all the paynims murmured: "This well may be that he saith."

5

So hath Marsila resolved him, and now to his side doth he call
Clargis the lord of Balgherra, and Estramariz withal;
And Eudropin his vassal and Priam the summons heard,
And Baciel and Guarlan of the reverend snowy beard;
Maheu his uncle, Johunel, Malprant from far overseas,
And Blancandrin, to lay before them his counsel's mysteries—
Even ten of his falsest caitiffs, and thus he spake unto these:
"Hear now, my lords and barons: ye shall go unto Charlemagne.
Even now he besiegeth Cordova the royal city of Spain.
Green branches of the olive in suppliant hands bear ye,
To be for a sign and a token of peace and humility.
And if ye by your subtle wisdom may set us twain at accord,
Red gold enow will I give you and silver for your reward,
Broad lordships and fiefs moreover so much as each man would."
Answered the paynim barons: "The word of our lord is good."

6

Marsila the King hath resolved him: his council now hath an end.
And he spake to his men: "Lords barons, now on your way shall ye wend.
Branches green of the olive let each man bear in hand,
And before King Charlemagne, bearing this my message, stand:
By the name of his God beseech him to have compassion on me;
And, or ever he seeth the passing of this month forth, say ye,

I—2

I will follow him, I and a thousand of the lords of my fealty,
There by the rite baptismal the Christian faith to embrace,
And to be in love his vassal and in loyalty all my days.
Touching hostages, if he require them, he shall verily have enow."
And spake Blancandrin : "A treaty full fair shalt thou compass so."

7

Then gave the King commandment, and ten white mules brought they
By Sicilia's king to Marsila sent overseas on a day.
Their bridle-reins were golden, their saddles with silver shone ;
And they that should bear his message, his ten lords, mounted thereon.
They bare in their hands green branches plucked from the olive-trees,
For this is the paynims' token of humility and peace.
So unto Charlemagne rode they, who hath fair France in his sway—
Ah me ! they shall somewhat beguile him to his hurt, let him do what he may !

8

The Emperor Charles is in spirit blithe, and of courage high.
He hath taken the city Cordova, her ramparts shattered lie ;
He hath dashed with his great war-engines her towers to the dust from the sky.
Abundance of costly treasure his knights have won for a prey,
Great wealth of gold and silver, and passing-rich array.
In all that city remaineth no living pagan now
Save such as have taken upon them our faith's baptismal vow.
King Charlemagne is seated in an orchard great and fair,
And there at his side is Roland, and Oliver is there ;
Sansun the battle-leader, Anseïs the proud thereto,
And the King's own banner-bearer, Geoffrey the lord of Anjou.
Otho the warrior greybeard, Count Berenger there may ye see,
Duke Naimes, and Engelier ruler of Burdel's seignory,
And Garnier and Anselm, and Guy of Gascony.
And there was the bold peer Gerin, and his comrade Gerier :
Ay, many more beside them of that great company were,
Franks fifteen thousand, children of France the sweet and fair.
All round be the good knights sitting on fair white silken pall ;

They be casting the dice at the tables to make them sport withal.
Before the chessboard seated is many an old wise knight,
While the swords in the hands of the younger are flashing in mimic fight.
Under a tall dark pine-tree, beside an eglantine,
Of purest gold wrought wholly doth the throne royal shine.
Thereon sitteth he who ruleth sweet France with kingly power:
His beard is white as the snowdrift, his head as the almond-flower;
Goodly his form is, his visage filled with majesty.
If a stranger fain would behold him, none needeth to say, "This is he!"
—Lo, come Marsila's envoys: from the saddles they leap to their feet,
And they bow them in salutation, as for love and homage meet.

9

Blancandrin before Charles stayeth his feet in front of the rest,
And first before his fellows himself hath he addressed
To greet the King, and with courtly obeisance he speaketh the word:
"Emperor, righteous ruler, blessed be thou of the Lord,
The God who made the heavens, the earth, and the depths of the sea,
And who gave his body to suffer on the cross long agony,
Who from pains of hell to deliver our souls did his life outpour:
Even him, and none beside him, behoveth us to adore.
Here sendeth to you his greeting Marsila the royal knight:
He hath heard of the Way of Salvation, he hath earnestly searched for the light,
And he wills to become a Christian, if it seemeth thee meet and right.
Unto you of his royal possessions rich gifts shall be sent of my King:
Bears and lions and sleuth-hounds in leash unto thee will we bring,
With costly steeds fleet-footed and strong, for our prince's gift,
Seven hundred camels, a thousand falcons moulted and swift.
Four hundred strong mules laden with silver and gold shall be there,
And money so much as fifty treasure-wains may bear,
Such glittering store of bezants of fine gold tried in the fire,
That thereof thou shalt fully render to thy men of war their hire.
And he saith: 'O King, thou hast tarried so long in the land of Spain,
That well mayest thou turn backward to France and to Aix again.'
Himself will follow thee thither—my lord thus saith by me—

And there will receive baptism and the faith that is holden of thee.
He shall swear him thy vassal, laying joined hands in the hands of his chief,
And shall hold henceforth the kingdom of Spain of thee in fief,
And shall render thee lowly service and loyal through all his days."
Then Charles our lord made answer: "Unto God be all the praise!
Nothing can I claim further, when such great debt he pays!"
Thereat the Emperor lifteth his hands unto God on high;
Then boweth his visage earthward, pondering earnestly.

10

Awhile sat the Emperor musing, and nought the bowed head stirred:
He was never hasty to utter the unreturning word;
His wont was long to linger ere he spake his thought aloud;
But his face at the last hath he lifted, and his look is high and proud;
And he answered the paynim envoys: "Ye have spoken exceeding well;
But this your King Marsila is mine enemy fierce and fell.
Now, as touching the words ye have spoken, or ever I take rede,
Say, what shall be my warrant that the word shall become the deed?"
"With hostages will we pledge us," answered the Saracen:
"Thou shalt have ten—nay, if it please thee, fifteen, yea, twice ten;
And, to hold his life at thy mercy, with these will I send my son,
And, save of the blood of our noblest, among them all shall be none.
And when unto Aix returning thou shalt stand in thy royal hall,
And unto Saint Michael of Peril shalt hold high festival,
My King Marsila willeth to follow thee thitherward;
And there, in the great baths fashioned for thee by Heaven's Lord,
By holy rite baptismal unto Christ will he be sealed."
Spake Charles: "The way of salvation unto him may yet be revealed!"

11

By this was the sun slow-sinking to a golden evenfall;
And King Charles gave commandment to stable the mules in stall;
And he bade men rear a pavilion within that orchard wide,
And he caused Marsila's heralds ten therein to abide.
Ten pursuivants he appointed to guard them through the night;

So there through the darkness they tarried till again the day shone bright.
From his bed hath the Emperor risen while yet the dawn is dim;
And the King hath heard the mass-chant, and the holy matin-hymn.
Then forth he passeth, and sitteth beneath a pine the King,
And he sendeth his hest to his barons to come to the council-ring;
For all that he doth he doeth by the Frank peers' counselling.

12

On the rosy feet of the morning doth the sun unclouded shine;
And Charles the mighty hath hied him to his place beneath the pine;
And now on the throne he sitteth of pure gold under its shade.
His barons have heard his summons, and now is the council arrayed.
Duke Naimes the Lord of Baviers was the first that his call obeyed:
Here is the Danes' Duke Ogier, Archbishop Turpin withal:
Richard the aged and Henri of Galney have hearkened the call,
And Thierry—brother to Geoffrey the Angevin Count is he;
Tedbald of Reims and Milo his cousin there may ye see,
And Gerier, one with Gerin in love and in constancy.
And lo, mid the great assembly, Roland the Count is here,
And Oliver beside him, a valiant and noble peer.
Yea, here be more than a thousand Franks for France which have fought.
And there that Ganelon cometh, of whom was the treason wrought;
Ay, out of that hour's counsel was deadliest evil brought.

13

Spake Charles the Emperor: "Barons, give ear unto me, my lords.
In council speak for my profit, yea, for your own, your words.
Messengers King Marsila hath sent, be it known unto you:
He is fain of his royal possessions to give rich gifts not a few:
Bears hath he sent, and lions, and hounds leashed two and two;
Horses of price, fleet-footed war-steeds goodly to see;
Seven hundred camels, a thousand mewed falcons sendeth he;
Four hundred strong mules laden with gold of Araby,
And bezants so much as fifty treasure-wains may bear.
But—but he maketh conditions, that back unto France I fare:

Thereafter to Aix, to my palace, will he follow me, he saith,
And receive by the rite baptismal salvation through our faith,
And be made a Christian: his marches in fief shall he hold of me;
And, so long as life endureth, my servant shall he be.
Hostages ten, yea, twenty, for surety proffereth he.
Howbeit, what purpose he hideth within him, nowise I know."
"We must needs be exceeding wary!" the Frank lords murmured low.

14

So made he an end of speaking. To his feet Count Roland sprang.
He abhorred that counsel: clashing against it his voice outrang:
"O righteous lord, all trusting in the word of Marsila were vain!
Full seven years have passed over since we entered the land of Spain.
I have won for thee Morinda and Nobles by this right hand:
I have taken the burg Valterra, have given thee Pina's land:
Balgherra hath fallen, Tudela is thine, and royal Seville;
Aulert on the Spanish marches, and Pont on its castled hill.
But for this Marsila—a traitor he was, and is traitor still.
Unto thee of his infidel liars sent he not once fifteen,
Each man in his false hand bearing a bough of the olive green?
And the selfsame words did they bring thee: a council didst thou call
Of thy Franks; and pitiful counsel they gave thee—fools were they all!
And so of thine earls thou sentest twain—for the paynim to slay!
Basàn fared forth at thy bidding to his death with Basile that day;
For he shore their heads from their shoulders under the walls of Haltaye!
Now nay, let the war speed forward whereto thou hast set thine hand.
To the fortress Saragossa lead thou thy warrior-band;
Besiege it—yea, though the leaguer should last thine whole life through—
Until thou hast gotten vengeance for those whom the felon slew."

15

There with bowed head unmoving Charles sat, perplexèd sore:
At his beard he plucked, and the knightly fringe of his lips he tore,
The while to his nephew he answered no word of bad or good.
And all the Franks kept silence, till Ganelon forth stood;

For he sprang to his feet, forth striding he came before the King,
And his mien was exceeding haughty, and loud did the scorn of him ring:
"To give ear to a fool in his folly," he cried, "right ill were it done—
Be it I or another—take counsel of thine own profit alone.
Seeing that King Marsila his promise to thee hath sent
To become thy vassal, with claspèd hands at thy footstool bent,
And to hold all Spain by tenure of fief, his liege-lord thou,
And unto our faith to seal him by holy baptismal vow—
Now therefore, whoso adviseth that we thrust such proffer by,
My lord King, little he recketh by what deaths all we die!
Let counsels of pride with their glamour no longer delude our. eyes.
Leave we the fools to their folly; henceforth let us hold by the wise."

16

Before the King thereafter Naimes the reverend rose:
His head was the almond in blossom, his beard was the drifted snows.
Never a better vassal in Charlemagne's presence stood.
He spake to the King: "This counsel that now ye have heard is good,
Even the words of the answer that Ganelon giveth the King.
Wise be they—if good understanding fail not for their following.
Marsila the King hath been vanquished—yea, is as good as dead:
His castles all have been taken, so well thine arms have sped:
Battered by thy war-engines his walls have crumbled to dust:
Burned be his cities, and earthward his donjon-keeps have been thrust.
When he sendeth and pleadeth for mercy in his hour of bitter need,
To trample on the fallen were surely an evil deed.
Send to him therefore a baron of these that wait at thy side,
By whom of his heart's true purpose we so may be certified.
If with hostages he will bind him to make the word the deed,
It is meet that in war wide-wasting this land no more should bleed."
Low murmured the Franks: "Right wisely the Duke hath uttered his rede."

17

"Lords, counsel me: who shall be chosen," said Charles, "on our mission to fare,
Mine answer to King Marsila in Saragossa to bear?"

And the old Duke Naimes made answer: "I am ready at thy command;
Deliver the royal gauntlet and the herald's staff to mine hand."
But the Emperor straightway lifted his head, and he answered him: "No!
That will I not: thy wisdom in counsel I cannot forego.
By the fringe that my lips overdroopeth, by my white beard sweeping low,
Thou shalt not at this season remove thee so far from me.
Nay, sit thou down: to the mission hath no man summoned thee."

18

Then spake he: "Who shall be chosen to utter our royal will
To the Saracen, who holdeth Saragossa the fortress still?"
Then spake and answered Roland: "Lo, ready to go stand I!"
"Not a foot shalt thou stir, of a surety!" did the good Count Oliver cry.
"So fiery-hot is thy spirit, the words of thy mouth so stout,
Thou wouldst do thyself and thy mission a mischief, sorely I doubt.
Myself will go full gladly, if this be the mind of my King.
If thou will it, myself more meetly can serve thee in this thing."
Then bowed was the head of his liege-lord in silent pondering.
At the last he spake and answered: "Keep silence, thou and thou,
Forasmuch as of you twain neither shall be mine herald now;
For I swear by the beard that hath whitened in sight of you all through the years,
I will doom not unto the peril any of these Twelve Peers."
Not a Frank made answer: his sentence in silence the multitude hears.

19

Yet after a space stepped Turpin of Reims from the council-ring.
In a great voice clear-ringing he cried unto Charles the King:
"O righteous King, henceforward let these thy Franks know peace.
Seven years in the land have they tarried warring without surcease,
Enduring sore tribulation and travail of weariful days.
Commit unto me thy gauntlet, the staff let mine hand raise,
And I will go thine herald to the Saracen lord of Spain,
And from speaking to him what seemeth me good not I will refrain.
So will I search out his purpose, and prove if in deeds he be true."
But the Emperor kindled to anger made answer thereunto:

"By my beard, and afar wouldst thou leave me?—nothing thereof shalt thou do!
Go, on the silk white-woven sit thee down as before,
And, except I give commandment, open thy lips no more!"

20

"Ye knights of France, advise me," said the Emperor yet again;
"Unto you I commit it—choose ye a baron of my domain,
One who to King Marsila with discretion my message shall say,
And who, if need be, hath valour to guard his life in the fray."
Laughed Roland: "Discretion with valour?—this shall be Ganelon!
None hast thou among thy barons of whom it were better done."
Loud cried the Franks consenting: "None more discreet we know!
If such be the King's good pleasure, meet is it that he should go."

21

"Ganelon, step thou forward; receive the staff," said his lord,
"And the gauntlet. Lo, thou hast heard it: the Franks with one accord
Judge that to Saragossa thou bear to the king my word."
"Not they, Sire!" Ganelon answered; "but Roland hath wrought this thing!
I will hate him with bitterest hatred my whole life through, O King!
Here, in thy very presence, at him my defiance I fling!
And Oliver his comrade in this mine hate hath share,
Yea, and the Twelve Peers also, for the love that to Roland they bear!
And if from this Saracen Spaniard ever alive I return,
In this same year on the plotters shall the flame of mine anger burn."
"Unrighteous is thy despiteful spirit," answered his lord.
"Of a surety, thither thou goest, since I have spoken the word."
"Sir King, at thy commandment," said Ganelon, "thither I fare—
O yea, I may go! but surety of life is none for me there,
As none had Basàn and his brother Basile, who found death's snare.

22

Well know I, to Saragossa I cannot choose but go;
But the man who journeyeth thither shall never return, I trow.
King, thou shouldst never have trusted Roland and his pride!

Thine whole realm into ruin and wrack would he fain misguide.
Remember, Sire, thy sister whom thou gavest to wife unto me;
Remember the son she hath borne me: on earth none fairer may be.
If he live to be man, my Baldwin, true knight shall he be and bold.
Unto him I bequeath my lordships, and the fiefs that of thee I hold;
Watch over him well, on whom never again mine eyes shall rest!"
Spake Charles: "Unmeet such softness is for a brave man's breast!
Thou must needs fare forth on the mission, since this is thy King's behest."

23

Thereat with bitter anguish was Ganelon's spirit wrung.
He strode unto Roland; a prideful glance at the hero he flung.
Earthward he cast the ermine cloak from his shoulders that hung,
And he stood in his silken doublet, grey-eyed and haughty-faced,
Goodly of form, as a deerhound slender in hip and waist,
But mighty of limb, broad-shouldered, that all men marvelling gazed.
"Thou felon!" he cried unto Roland, "what madness in thee doth dwell?
Into thy body have entered living fiends of hell!
Ha, when the Franks take counsel, thy work they well may arraign,
For day by day thou loadest upon them travail and pain!
Still for thine own good only thou houndest them on to the fray.
Our Emperor Charles first knew thee, in truth, in an evil day;
For by thy pride of spirit, and by thy treacherous mood,
Of me not alone dost thou rob him, but of barons many and good.
I am thy mother's husband, as thy jealous heart doth know,
And for this cause so hast thou plotted that I to Marsila go.
But if I return, shall mischief requite thee!—sorrow and bane
Will I render to thee, that shall last thee so long as thy life shall remain!"
Answered him Roland: "O folly and pride! These know that I dread
No threats—but the words of a ruler by lips of the wise should be said:
I then, if it please my liege-lord, am ready to go in thy stead."

24

"And wouldst *thou* go," Ganelon answered, "for me?—that shalt thou not!
What, man, thou art not my vassal, nor I thy lord, I wot.

Charles hath commanded: his service by none save me must be wrought.
Yea, and myself am wholly willing his message to bear.
To the city Saragossa and Marsila hence will I fare,
To the place whither no man goeth but leaveth his life in the snare.
But and if I return peradventure, if God my life shall spare,
Then—then will I remember! Some mad work yet will I make,
When I deal with these co-plotters who have doomed me to this for thy sake,
Ere the flame be quenched of my fury, ere the fire of mine anger I slake!"
At Ganelon's wild words Roland into scornful laughter brake.

25

When Ganelon heard that laughter of Roland, anguish-filled
Was his heart unto bursting: his senses on the verge of madness reeled;
And he cried to the Count: "In hatred I hold thee for ever and aye!
Thou hast caused an unjust sentence to light upon me this day!
Emperor, fountain of justice, here in thy presence I stand;
Give thou straightway the gauntlet and the herald's staff to mine hand.
Ready am I to accomplish all thine high command.
But if ever God of his mercy vouchsafe me safe return,
Not long shall it tarry, the vengeance for the which mine heart doth yearn!"
Spake Charles: "Without reason or justice doth the flame of thine anger burn."

25 a

Yet again said the King: "No longer, Ganelon, here must thou stay.
To the paynim in Saragossa get thee forth on thy way.
From me unto King Marsila say: if he will to embrace
Our Faith, he must swear him my vassal, his hands 'twixt mine must he place.
One half of Spain thereafter will I give him, in fief to hold
Of me, and half by Roland my baron shall be controlled.
If this my pact be rejected, I will lead my war-array
Unto Saragossa, and cease not till I have taken the prey.
In his own despite will I seize him, his feet in fetters lay;
Unto Aix the royal city shall he be haled straightway.
We will doom him there to the headsman for his deeds of evil fame,
And there shall he pass in torment to his end, and in utterest shame.

Take thou with thee this letter in the which is all enscrolled,
And thyself in his right hand lay it, that nought may be left untold."

26

Then Charles held forth the gauntlet of his right hand with the word;
But Ganelon faltered—the craven had fain been afar from his lord!—
When the Emperor looked he should take it, betwixt them it fell to the earth;
And the Franks at the deed unfeatly were somewhat moved unto mirth.
Ganelon stoopeth him earthward, that glove from the ground to raise:
Well-nigh distraught is the baron for shame and confusion of face.
In his heart to the God of Glory who sitteth in Heaven he prayed
To destroy the men by whose dooming he accounted himself betrayed.
"God! what shall betide of this omen?" murmured the Frankish peers.
"'Tis a presage of loss and of sorrow!" they whispered with boding fears.
"My lords," said Ganelon, "tidings thereof shall come to your ears."

27

And he spake yet again: "My liege-lord, grant to me leave to be gone.
Since I needs must depart, I have nothing to do to linger on."
"Go then: in the name of Jesus and mine be thy task essayed."
The sign of absolution above him his right hand made,
And therewith the scroll of the letter and the staff in his hand he laid.
So Ganelon thence departeth to prepare for his wayfaring;
And a hundred his knights attend him from the presence of the King,
Men who will never forsake him, neither for treasure nor gold.
But hot with indignation is the Count, and angry-souled;
And the deadly work of his hatred full soon shall the Franks behold.

28

Now to his own pavilion Count Ganelon hath passed,
And his goodliest vesture and armour he searcheth out in haste.
The golden spurs hath he buckled to his heels, he girds to his side
The brand Morglay, and the war-horse Tachebrun doth he bestride.
The saddle was silver-broidered, and gold-bestarred was the rein,
And all his charger's housings were cloth of costly grain.

Held for him was the stirrup by his uncle Guinemer's hand.
"Sire, let us companion thy journey!" cried they of his vassal-band.
"Now God the Lord forbid it," Ganelon answered again,
"That ye unto Saragossa should ride in a doomed man's train!
Better alone that I perish, than that knights so many be slain!
And if I there shall be murdered, and thereof one bring you word,
Ye shall cause that masses be chanted for the peace of the soul of your lord.
To sweet France after a season, my dear lords, shall ye fare,
And on that day this my greeting to my dear wife shall ye bear,
And unto my friend and companion, the good peer Pinabel,
And unto my young son Baldwin: of a surety ye know him well.
Ever do ye defend him, and guard his lordships aye."
Then Ganelon turned him, and forward he rode on his fatal way.
Many a knightly vassal might ye see sore weeping there,
And a great and bitter crying at his parting rent the air.
Then said they: "An ill day, baron, is this that to thee doth befall!
Long time hast thou stood in presence of our King in camp and hall;
And all men needs must acclaim thee his noblest vassal of all.
We will hate him ever whose plotting for thee this journey decreed!
How dared he, this Count Roland, devise such caitiff deed
Against thee, who by lineage comest of such high princely seed?
He shall not be upheld nor defended by all King Charlemagne's power
That he shall not be slain, or delivered to shame, in our vengeance-hour!"

29

Onward beneath the olives tall Count Ganelon rode
Till he came where the Saracen envoys yet his coming abode.
So set they forth on their journey; but behind that retinue
With Ganelon lingered Blancandrin: each close unto other they drew;
And with subtlety full wary together commune these two.
Blancandrin saith: "A wondrous hero is Charlemagne:
Rome hath he conquered, Apulia, Calabria, mountain and plain:
He hath ta'en Constantinople, and Saxony the wide,
And unto the land of the Angles hath he passed the salt sea-tide,
And tribute for the service of Saint Peter hath wrung therefrom.

But by this is he old; of his summers two hundred were surely the sum.
Now in quest of what to the marches of this our land hath he come?"
Said Ganelon: "This is the answer—such is his pleasure still,
And none shall be found so mighty as to countervail his will."

30

"Right valiant," said Blancandrin, "be the Franks; I gainsay it nought:
Yet oft by your counts and your war-dukes is grievous mischief wrought
To their lord, such evil counsel still do they give to their King,
To heap on him travail, and ruin on many beside they bring."
And Ganelon said: "Of a surety none other man can I name
Of whom this may be said, save Roland: all his is the sin and the shame.
Our Emperor yester-morning was sitting beneath the shade,
And around was a great throng gathered of the knights of his battle-aid,
When strode his nephew before him, yet in his hauberk arrayed;
From all round Carcassone had he gathered war-spoil in;
And there in his hand was he bearing an apple scarlet of skin.
'Lo there, fair Sire,' to his uncle the King did Roland say,
'The crowns of all kings conquered thus at thy feet I lay!'
Of a surety his arrogant spirit shall work his ruin yet!
Not a day but on the hazard of death his life is set.
Ah, were he slain!—for only his fall our peace should beget."

31

And Blancandrin said: "This Roland is a passing ruthless lord,
Who would humble all kings of all nations into thraldom to the sword,
And would lay the hand of the spoiler on all lands near and far!
Say by what helpers he thinketh to achieve such deeds of war."
"By all the Franks," made answer the knight: "in very deed
So well do they love him that never they fail him in his need;
For gold he gives them for guerdon, he lavishes silver withal,
Gives mules and battle-horses, rich armour and silken pall.
And as for the Emperor—howso he pleaseth he turneth him still.
But, for this thy counsel, in no wise may he be won to thy will.
He will march his conquering armies through all Spain, so doth he boast,

And thereafter to Babylon's ramparts will lead his unresting host,
And Baligant the Emir there, saith he, will he slay,
Except he receive baptism, and the law of Christ obey.
Yea, onward and onward ever will he stretch his victorious hand,
Till he conquer the whole world's compass from here to the Morning-land."
The Saracen glanced at him keenly: he thought, "'Tis a goodly man
With a felon's eye!"—and a shiver through Ganelon's whole frame ran:
Then the infidel spake and answered: "Give ear unto me," he said:
"Wouldst avenge thee on Roland? Betray him to us: by Mahound, he is dead!
Right courteous our King is, and treasures untold shall he lavish on thee."
Ganelon hearkens and hearkens, with brows drooped heavily.

32

So side by side rode onward Blancandrin and Ganelon
Communing, till each of other a pledge by oath had won
To rest not from traitorous plotting till Roland to death were done.
By highways and byways onward ever rode these two,
Till at last at Saragossa they drew rein 'neath a yew.
A cloth of the white silk woven on the green grass lay, and thereon
Of pure gold fashioned wholly was set a kingly throne;
And thereon was the dark king sitting who held the marches of Spain,
With Saracens twenty thousand around him, a royal train.
And from all that array no murmur, no least sound, stirred the air,
So eager for the tidings that now drew nigh they were.
And lo, they beheld Blancandrin and Ganelon standing there.

33

In the presence now of Marsila the King doth Blancandrin stand;
With Ganelon he cometh, and he holdeth the Count by the hand;
And he maketh beginning of speaking with words of fairest sound,
As he giveth his master greeting: "Blessed be thou of Mahound
And Apollo, to whom in service and faith all we are bound!
We bare unto Charles thy message: he lifted his hands unto heaven,
And thanked his God: none answer beside unto me hath he given;
But he sendeth you hither a baron of them which stand in his sight,

W. C. R.   2

A lord of France, and a chieftain of exceeding honour and might.
From his lips shall ye hear the decision of his king, be it peace or war."
"Let him speak," made answer Marsila, "ready to hear we are."

34

Now well had Ganelon pondered, and as one whom wisdom doth lead
To speak the word in season, so spake he with good heed;
And thus to the King he crieth: "Blessed be thou of the Lord,
The glorious God who claimeth of men to be adored!
Lo, this is Charlemagne's message—unto thee that warrior saith:
Thou by the rite baptismal must receive our Christian faith:
Thou must swear thee his vassal, laying joined hands in the hands of thy chief.
Then half of Spain he consenteth to grant thee to hold in fief
Of him, and half by Roland his baron shall be controlled—
If thou have him to thy co-regent, thou shalt find him masterful-souled!
And if this his pact be rejected, he will lead his war-array
Unto Saragossa; till falleth into his hands the prey,
Will he cease not his leaguer, will seize thee, in fetters thy feet will he lay:
Unto Aix the royal city shalt thou be haled straightway.
They will doom thee there to the headsman for thy deeds of evil fame;
And there shalt thou pass in torment to thine end, and in utterest shame."
When Marsila heard, above measure was the wrath that upon him came:
With a sudden shiver of fury did he tremble through all his frame:
The form of his visage was altered, the colour thereof was gone;
And in wrathful indignation he rose up from his throne.
As it chanced, in his hand was he holding a golden-feathered dart:
Had his councillors not withheld him, he had hurled it at Ganelon's heart.

35

From the face of the King Marsila all its colour fled;
In the grasp of his hand the javelin quivered, at point to be sped.
Ganelon marked it: he graspeth his sword, he draweth it there
To the half of its length from the scabbard—"Sword, thou art bright and fair!
While I bear thee in yonder presence, mine Emperor shall not say
That I died alone in the alien's land! Your best shalt pay
For my blood!" "Nay, part them!" shouted the lords of the paynim array.

36

Hot with exceeding anger was King Marsila then;
But so greatly they reproached him, the chief of the Saracen men,
That grudgingly he consented on his throne to seat him again.
Then spake unto him the Caliph: "Full evilly had we sped
If thou hadst fulfilled thy purpose to strike yon Frank lord dead.
Rather shouldst thou have hearkened till all his message were said."
"I must bear as I may this outrage, Sir King," Count Ganelon cried;
"But, by Saint Peter, who Romeward on God's great mission hied,
No fear of death shall withhold me; I will not turn aside
Nor refrain me, for all the abundance of wealth that is found in thy land,
From speaking, while yet I am suffered here in thy presence to stand,
The word that Charlemagne, mighty in kingly majesty,
Hath put in my mouth, to utter to his mortal enemy!"
A mantle of fur of the sable on his shoulders Ganelon wore,
And silk in the land of Egypt woven covered it o'er:
He cast it to earth, and Blancandrin received it as it fell;
But his sword would he not surrender to any infidel.
By the pommel of gold his right hand gripped it, defying death.
"A noble baron!" murmured the paynims under their breath.

37

One stride took Ganelon forward, and facing the King stood he;
And he cried unto him: "Thou hast little to do to be wroth with me!
If mischief befall thee, beseems thee to bear it patiently.
Lo, I speak yet again my message: the lord of all France saith
That thou by the rite baptismal must receive our Christian faith,
And become his loyal vassal: thine hands 'twixt his must thou fold;
Then half of Spain he consenteth to give thee, in fief to hold
Of him, and half by Roland his nephew shall be controlled—
If thou have him to thy co-regent, thou shalt find him masterful-souled!
And, if this pact be rejected, he will come to beleaguer thee
In Saragossa, till rifted before him her ramparts be.
In grasp of might will he seize thee, thy feet in fetters will lay:

2—2

Unto Aix the royal city shalt thou be haled straightway.
Thou shalt have nor palfrey nor war-steed, nor mule to ride thereon,
But across the back of a sorry sumpter-beast shalt be thrown,
And shalt lose thine head by sentence of the Franks' stern judgment-ring.
Lo, here mine Emperor's letter that saith it to thee do I bring."
He laid the scroll, as he spake it, in the right hand of the King.

38

Now Marsila the King was learnèd in all manner of clerkly lore,
Yea, oft on the holy writings of heathendom would he pore.
Still writhen with wrath was his visage, and leaden-pale of hue,
As he brake the seal of the letter, as the wax aside he threw,
As he looked upon the writing till the tenor thereof he knew.
Then tears from his eyes came rushing, his snow-white beard he tare;
He sprang to his feet, his indignant cry thrilled all the air:
"Hearken, my lords, with what deadly folly of arrogance
Charles layeth on me his commandment, this lord of the land of France
He calleth to my remembrance his wrath for Basàn and Basile
Whose heads I smote from their shoulders beneath Haltaia's hill.
If therefore now I would ransom mine head for that my deed,
I must send to him straightway the Caliph, my mother's brother's seed
Forasmuch as in slaying the envoys I hearkened to his rede.
If I do not this, my foeman is he to my latest day."
Not a word spake any heathen in that hush of pale dismay,
Till sprang to his feet that Caliph, and in grim wrath-shivering tone,
"Presumptuous folly," he shouted, "hath been uttered of Ganelon!
Such malapert words hath he spoken that he meriteth not to live!
Unto me deliver him: justice at mine hand shall he receive!"
When Ganelon heard that saying, on high he swung his brand,
And he set his back to a pine-tree, and facing his foes did he stand.

39

So there in Saragossa a stormy tumult roared.
But it chanced that a certain champion was there, a noble lord,
The son of a prince of the people, a mighty and valiant peer;

And now a counsel of wisdom he spake in his liege-lord's ear:
"Fair Sire, be nowise troubled: no hero or martyr is here.
The man is at heart a traitor: see his face—it is pallid with fear."
Then by command of Marsila that scroll on the flames did they fling.
"My lords, for a space here tarry," to his paynims said the King,
"While I go apart with my princes for secret counselling."
Then to a throne 'neath an olive set did Marsila go,
Whereunder was spread a silken cloth as white as snow,
And the wisest of his princes to commune with him did he bring.
There stood his uncle the Caliph amidst of the council-ring,
And Falsaron his brother and ally faithful and true,
And his son, the heir to his lordships, even Jorfaleu;
And Valdabrun, Malprimès, Moreïs and Climborin,
Clargis the lord of Balgherra, and white-haired Blancandrin,
Who said to the King: "To thy presence summon the Frank lord now,
For to help our cause hath he pledged him to me by oath and vow."
"Even so," made answer the Caliph, "thou bring him before the throne."
So thence that Saracen hasted where Ganelon stood alone,
And the traitor's right hand clasped he, its fingers he twined in his own,
And he whispered, "Come to Marsila, for now the truth is known."
So into the orchard he drew him: before the King he came,
There to commune of treason, to do the deed of shame.

40

Then spake unto him Marsila: "My fair lord Ganelon,
I make confession that folly of me unto thee was done
When I lifted mine hand as to smite thee, for the wrath that burned in me.
Lo now, with this mantle of ermine do I make amends unto thee.
Fresh from the hands of the cunning artificer came it to-day:
Scarce should a hundred pieces of gold the price of it pay."
Round the neck of the Count that mantle even with the word cast he;
And he seated him beside him beneath the olive-tree.
"Right fair amends," said the paynim, "for all will I make unto thee."
"Full willingly I accept it," Ganelon straightway said:
"God, if it be his pleasure, shall requite thy bountihead."

41

Thereafter spake Marsila: "Ganelon, hold it for sooth—
It is in mine heart to love thee in faithfulness and truth.
Now let this counsel, I pray thee, be secret between us twain.
And, first, fain am I to hear thee tell of Charlemagne:—
He is stricken in years of a surety, his good days long since fled:
By this two hundred winters, I ween, have whitened his head.
He hath dragged through many a kingdom his feet in his glory-quest,
Made many great kings beggars, of their kingdoms dispossessed.
Surely at Aix in Frankland now at the last might he rest!"
But Ganelon made answer: "Nay, Charles is of no such mould!
Not a man hath learnt to know him, of them which daily behold,
Who would not say that a hero is the Emperor his lord.
A splendour of chivalry over his brows our God hath poured.
Myself not enough can commend him, nor tell out all his praise,
Nor tell of his knightly honour, and all his royal grace;
And the tale of his dauntless valour, what tongue may tell it o'er?
Far liever would I perish than be baron of his no more!"

42

Spake yet again the paynim: "I needs must marvel sore
At Charlemagne: he is stricken in years, his head is hoar,
And by this with two hundred winters the leaf of his summer is sere.
He hath dragged his frame through many a country far and near,
Many a thrust hath he taken of lance, and push of spear,
Made many great kings beggars of their kingdoms dispossessed.
Say, when will he be weary of the endless glory-quest?"
"While liveth his nephew, never," said Ganelon, "shall this be.
'Neath the canopy of heaven is no such vassal as he.
A mighty champion moreover is his comrade Oliver,
And the Twelve Peers too, which be holden of Charlemagne full dear.
These be but the vanguard-leaders of twenty thousand more:
Secure in their might, Charles feareth no man the wide world o'er."

43

Yet again as before said the paynim: "Sorely I marvel at this,
Seeing Charlemagne's hair is whitened, and silver-hoary he is,
And a gulf of years two hundred, I ween, his life hath spanned:
He hath ridden in march triumphant through many and many a land.
Many a spear keen-pointed hath shocked against his shield;
Many a king most mighty hath he slain in stricken field.
When will he rest from warring, when to the years will he yield?"
"While Roland liveth, never," said Ganelon, "shall this be.
From here to the Land of the Morning is no such vassal as he.
A mighty champion, moreover, is his comrade Oliver,
And the Twelve Peers too, which be holden of Charlemagne full dear:
And they be but the vanguard-leaders of twenty thousand more;
And in arrogance their spirit and in pride so high doth soar,
Secure in their might, Charles feareth no man the wide world o'er.
But and if that pride might be humbled, should Charles grieve bitterly;
His right arm then should be broken, a hero no more should he be."

44

"But, my fair lord Ganelon," answered Marsila with wondering mien,
"I have men of war: more goodly warriors thou hast not seen:
Knights four hundred thousand my banners can lead to the fray.
Surely with these may I battle with Charles and his Frank array."
But Ganelon answered: "Thou canst not at this time compass the thing.
If thou make not pretence of submission to the Christian faith of the King,
Only to utter destruction thy paynim host wilt thou bring.
Put vain thoughts by, and hearken the counsel of the wise:
To the Emperor send such goodly presents, thy peace's price,
That all folk unto the story shall listen with wondering eyes.
And by these thy pledges persuaded, those hostages two-score,
Shall our King return to the pleasant land of France once more.
Yet mark—he will leave behind him a rearguard certainly,
And therein shall be Roland his nephew—for this will I answer, I—
And Oliver with him, a dauntless and courteous knight, shall remain.

Then, if thou wilt trust me touching the counts, dead men are the twain.
Yea, Charles shall behold his towered pride cast down to the dust:
He shall war never more against thee; we have quenched his battle-lust!

45

If once thy will be accomplished that Roland there lie slain,
It is even as though from the body of Charles were his right arm ta'en.
Little enow should avail him his marvellous hosts of war:
For the crown of gold that he weareth, its light shall be quenched evermore,
And the land of Spain shall slumber in peace from shore to shore."
Then fell on the neck of the traitor Marsila in loving wise:
He kissed him, and bade that his treasures be spread before his eyes.

46

"My fair lord Ganelon," answered the King Marsila again,
"How may the deed be accomplished that Roland shall be slain?"
"Even this will I show"—and the traitor unfolded all his guile:—
"Or ever the King ascendeth unto Sizra's huge defile,
He shall leave behind him a rearguard for his host's security,
And thereof his nephew Roland, the mighty count, shall be,
And Oliver beside him, whom he trusteth utterly.
Frank warriors twenty thousand shall be all their company.
Have thou thy great host mustered, and against them hurl at the first
Of thy paynims a hundred thousand: on those few down shall they burst;
And the ranks of France shall be mangled and rent in evil plight;
Yet I say not but many a warrior of thine shall die in the fight.
Then with a second war-host shalt thou clash with them in the strife:
Never shall Roland deliver from both of these his life!
So shalt thou have wrought a mighty deed of chivalry,
And war never more shall vex thee through all thy days to be."
And the King Marsila answered, "God's help be vouchsafed unto me!

47

"For words," then spake Marsila, "is there any further need?
What profit is there in counsel if it be not fulfilled in deed?

Fair sir, hear how I am minded to cause our purpose to speed:
Thou for betrayal of Roland make oath unto me straightway;
Swear thou that in the rearguard I shall surely find the prey,
And I on our holy writings unto thee will solemnly swear
That I surely will give battle to him, so I find him there;
And, except myself first perish, my sword shall smite him and slay."
And Ganelon said, "So be it, even as thou dost say."
He draweth off his gauntlet, and his right hand doth he lay
Upon the holy relics in the hilt of his sword Morglay:
He swore to the treason, and sealed him traitor from that day.

48

Now hard thereby was there standing a throne of ivory
With a white shield laid upon it, beneath an olive-tree.
Thereon Marsila commanded that a book be laid and unrolled
Wherein was the law of Mahomet and Tervagant enscrolled.
Thereon this Saracen Spaniard by an oath his soul hath bound
That if in the Frankish rearguard the body of Roland be found,
He will spare not to give him battle, will surely smite him and slay.
"Now fair befall our compact!" thereat did Ganelon say;
"Doomed are the Twelve Peers also by the covenant of this day."

49

Now cometh a certain paynim, Valdabrun, at whose side
Was the King Marsila knighted, and to Ganelon smiling he cried:
"My sword receive thou; a better hath no man on the earth.
'Twixt hilt and hilt lie gemstones of a thousand mangons' worth.
Fair sir, in token of friendship I give it, and for thine aid
Whereby we may find this Roland with the Franks' rearguard arrayed.
And I swear unto thee, we will surely fight with him to the death;
Ay, and I pledge mine honour that he it is who shall fall!"
"Now fair betide the issue!" unto him Count Ganelon saith.
Thereafter did each kiss other on cheek and on chin withal.

50

Then another lord of the paynims—Climborin named they his name—
To the traitor Ganelon, smiling the smile of friendship, came:
"Receive," he said, "mine helmet; none better shalt thou behold;
For its price were weighed in the balance four bezants of fine gold.
Lo, there upon the nose-guard doth a fiery ruby burn.
I give it to thee of friendship: I ask one thing in return,
That thou give us thine help in tangling Roland's feet in the snare,
That we may abase the honour of the Lord of the Marches there,
And bring down that vainglory, that pride beyond compare."
Thereto did Ganelon answer, "So may the issue befall!"
Thereafter did each kiss other on lips and on visage withal.

51

And now the Queen of Marsila, Bramimunde, drew near;
And she spake to the Count: "Sir baron, I hold thee passing dear.
On the lips of my lord and his servants thy praises have no end.
Lo here, to thy wife these bracelets, I pray thee, let me send.
With amethysts and with jacinths is the gold set plenteously:
There be no such costly gemstones in all Rome's treasury:
To your King hath it never befallen such goodly jewels to see.
And never a day shall greet thee, but bringeth a gift from me."
And Ganelon made answer: "We will render requital to thee."
And he took and bestowed in his hose-band the reward of iniquity.

52

Then summoned the King Sir Valdit, which kept his treasury-key—
There was found no man more agèd in Spain from sea to sea—
"The gifts for Charles appointed, have all been prepared of thee?"
"Yea, Sire," that lord made answer, "ready be all to thine hand.
Seven hundred camels laden with silver and gold there stand,
And twenty hostages, noblest of birth in all the land."
Then for yet more gifts for the traitor he bade that lord make quest
Through his treasures: thereafter he turned him to Ganelon; unto his breast

In exceeding loving fashion the traitor hath he pressed;
And he saith: "In lovingkindness ever to thee am I bound:
Never a day shall greet thee with gifts from me uncrowned,
So by thine help this Roland the champion to death be done."
"No need that thou urge me," he answered; "mine heart is set thereon."

53

His hand upon Ganelon's shoulder layeth Marsila now,
And he saith: "Thou art passing valiant, and passing wise art thou.
By the law of your God I beseech thee, wherein salvation ye find,
Have a care that nothing turn thee from this thy present mind!
Lo, of my wealth am I purposed to give without stint unto thee,
Gold, even seven mules' burden of the purest of Araby.
And never a year shall greet thee ungraced by the like from me.
Now take them, the keys of goodly Saragossa's rampart-ring;
And all these costly presents deliver thou to thy King;
Even whatso gifts I promised but now, unto him do thou bring.
And the hostages twenty deliver, of him to be kept in ward.
But in any wise doom thou Roland to be left with the Franks' rearguard.
If in mountain-gorge or in defile on him I may but light,
Then will I close in grapple with him of mortal fight."
He answered, "Meseemeth I linger all too long by this."
So he gat him to horse, and in short space far on his journey he is.

54

By this to his conquered kingdom the Emperor draweth nigh,
And over the burg Valterra already his banners fly.
That burg Count Roland had taken, had cast down rampart and tower,
And through seven long years deserted had it lain since that wild hour.
For tidings of Ganelon waiting there did the King remain,
And looked for the coming tribute of that great land of Spain.
It is morning, even the dayspring, as the eastward heaven grows bright,
When Ganelon down from his charger at his harbourage doth light.

55

Fair are the feet of the morning, and cloudless-bright is the sun:
With dawn hath the Emperor risen, and forth of his chamber is gone,
And hath heard the prayer of matins and the chanting of the mass,
And in front of his great pavilion is he standing now on the grass.
There in his presence was Roland, and valiant Oliver,
And Naimes the old war-leader, and others full many there were;
And thither Ganelon cometh, the felon knight forsworn,
And full of traitorous cunning are the words of his false heart born;
And he said to the King: "Now blessed be thou of the Lord this day,
The Creator, to whom it behoveth that we all homage pay!
The keys of Saragossa, lo, at thy feet I lay;
Full many a costly present bring I here to my Lord;
And here be hostages twenty: keep them safely in ward.
And the King Marsila maketh petition to thee by me
That in no wise shalt thou blame him that I bring not the Caliph to thee.
Mine eyes beheld him fleeing; a hundred thousand fled,
Saracens clad in hauberks, with helmet laced on head,
And a sword with golden pommel girded to each man's side:
All these took ship together with him on the Mid-sea tide.
Yea, I watched till their galleys were laden with that huge company.
All these in fear and abhorrence from the faith of Christ would fly,
So loth were they to receive it, and to keep its precepts high.
But scarce had they won to the outsea, as it were four leagues from the shore,
When there burst upon them a tempest with the storm-wind's mighty roar.
There are they drowned, and never shall eye behold them again.
Of a truth, if alive were the Caliph, I had brought him in my train.
And concerning the King of the paynims, this hold for verity:
Thou shalt not have seen the passing of the month´that draweth nigh,
Ere King Marsila shall follow thee unto thy realm of France,
To receive the faith of the Christian and the holy ordinance,
And to swear himself thy vassal, with clasped hands laid in thine,
And of thee to hold such kingdom in Spain as thou shalt assign,
And to render thee loyal service to his life's end evermore."

"Praise unto God and thanksgiving!" loud cried the Emperor:
"Well hast thou done, and goodly reward shalt thou have therefor."
Then blown were a thousand trumpets through all that host of war.
The Franks break up their encampment, their sumpter-beasts they load;
And to sweet France setting their faces have they taken the homeward road

56

The Emperor hath wasted all Spain in that long war;
He hath broken down her castles, in ruins her cities are;
But now he sayeth within him that the war is ended at last,
And to sweet France, yea, to the home-land, the Emperor rideth fast.
Lo, now is the long day waning, and evensong is nigh:
Count Roland hath planted his ensign on a hill that heaves to the sky,
And o'er all the land around him encamped doth the Frank host lie.
But ever the foe draw nearer by hidden gorge and vale:
Clad are they all in hauberks, in links of the knitted mail.
With helmets laced and with broadswords girt ride cavaliers;
Their shields from their necks are swinging: there be ranks of targeteers,
There be glittering points of javelins, and ordered lines of spears.
In a wood on the mountain's shoulder their host through the night-tide lies
There wait four hundred thousand till the light of the dayspring rise.
Ah God, what pity that hidden is all from the Frenchmen's eyes!

57

From the face of the earth day fleeteth, the pall of night drops down
And Charles in slumber lieth, that Emperor of renown.
Then dreamed he a dream that betided sorrow exceeding great;
For he thought that he stood at Sizra, the mountain rock-wall's gate,
And between his hands was he holding his lance of the ashwood tough
Then came to him Ganelon, laying his grasp on the shaft thereof.
So starkly did he wrench it, so mightily swing and shake,
That between his hands was it shivered, and all to fragments brake;
And lo, the gleaming splinters up to the heaven leap.
But Charles the King still slumbers, he wakeneth not from sleep.

58

Thereafter to that sleeper did another vision come;
And behold, in France was he standing, in Aix his royal home.
By two chains had he been holding for a little space a bear;
But it rose against him, and sorely the beast his right arm tare,
That even from the bone the mangled flesh by his fangs is ta'en.
Even then he beheld a leopard which came from the side of Spain;
And overagainst his body it crouched as in act to spring;
But forth of his palace-portal a hound came hastening
Which sped like the wind on-rushing with swift leaps thitherward,
And fought, as a knight might battle, for love of the King his lord.
By the right ear seized he the felon bear, and he tore it away;
Then with the leopard he grappled in fury of the fray.
And the sleeper heard voices crying, "Great battle and sore is at hand!"
Yet no Frank there divineth with whom shall the victory stand.
But Charles the King still sleepeth, unbroken is slumber's band.

59

But the night-tide swiftly passeth, and bright doth the morn's face beam,
And the Emperor Charles upstarteth from slumber and from dream.
Blithely a thousand war-horns are sounding clear and high;
And to horse the King gat straightway with all his chivalry.
"Lo now, my lords and barons," to his peers King Charlemagne cried,
"Behold these perilous passes and gorges on every side.
Judge ye for me what captain shall tarry to guard our rear."
Straight Ganelon cried: "Lo, Roland my stepson standeth here.
No baron for suchlike service thou hast who shall be his peer."
When the King heard that, he beheld him with glance indignant and stern,
And he spake: "In thy soul of a surety doth mortal hatred burn!
Into thy body have entered living fiends from hell!
Say thou then—who in the vanguard shall clear our way so well?"
But straightway Ganelon answered: "Ogier of Denmark is he:
Thou hast no baron of higher account in valiancy."

60

So soon as that decision by Roland the Count was heard,
Then, like a knight full knightly, he spake the answering word:
"Sir kinsman, thanks do I render with all my heart unto thee,
For that thou hast adjudged the honour of the rearguard unto me.
There is no man shall supplant me in the glory of this award,
And, with Roland's knowledge, shall nothing be lost to the King our lord,
No, not the worth of a denier, not a mule that man may ride,
Not a beast of the sorriest garrons that sumpter-varlets bestride,
But, save by payment in sword-strokes, the spoiler shall win it not."
And Ganelon answered: "Soothly thou speakest, well I wot."

61

Now when Count Roland bethought him by whose devising it came
That to him was the rearguard given, with sudden anger-flame
To his kinsman he cried: "Thou caitiff, from true knights' fellowship banned!
Didst deem that my good lord's gauntlet should slip to the earth from mine hand,
As fell from thy nerveless fingers in presence of Charles that wand?"

62

Unto Charles Count Roland hath turned him, and he crieth with scorn on the lip:
"Give to me, Sire, I pray thee, the bow that thou hast in thy grip.
I pledge thee my faith, no mortal shall for this on me cry shame,
That I let thy gage fall earthward, as befell when before thee came
Ganelon, when thy gauntlet and staff from his hand dropped down,
When thou badst him go to Marsila in Saragossa-town."
But his head the Emperor boweth, his snow-white beard perplexed
Doth he pluck, and he cannot refrain him to weep from a heart sore vexed.

63

Unto the King thereafter did Naimes the reverend go:
His head was the almond in blossom, his beard was the drifted snow.
Never a better vassal in Charlemagne's presence stood.
And he spake to the King: "Thou hast heard him; exceeding wrathful of mood

Is Roland the Count: his spirit is angered and passing grim.
Lo now, the charge of the rearguard hath been adjudged unto him:
There is none among all thy barons shall supplant him in this command;
Give to him therefore the war-bow which thou bearest in thine hand.
But see to it thou that thy warder have battle-helpers enow."
His hand the King outstretcheth, and Roland receiveth the bow.

64

Then spake the King unto Roland: "Now knowest thou all indeed,
Fair lord my nephew: the rearguard full knightly wilt thou lead.
Behold, the half of my war-host will I leave with thee to abide.
Gather them round thee: thy safety they are, if mischief betide."
Answered him Roland: "Never will I do such deed of shame!
May God Most High confound me, if I tarnish thus my name!
Frank heroes twenty thousand, no more, shall abide with me here.
Thou, pass through the mountain-gorges untroubled for thy rear:
So long as I live, no foeman shalt thou have cause to fear."

64 a

Now Roland the Count hath ascended to the top of a barrow green
Arrayed in the mail of his hauberk—better hath no man seen!
Laced on his head is his helmet; right well it becometh a knight!
No weapon forged may cleave it, how starkly soe'er one smite.
To his side is Durendal girded, the golden-hilted sword:
A shield from his neck is hanging that hath never failed its lord.
His spear on high hath he lifted with fluttering pennon white;
Low as his wrist are swinging the golden fringes bright.
In his armour arrayed he seemeth a passing goodly knight,
As on Veillantif mounted, his war-horse, he showeth against the sky.
And now the Count uplifteth his voice with a far-ringing cry:
"Now will I see who hateth, and see who loveth me!"
And the Franks with one voice shouted: "All we will follow thee!"

65

Proudly he stands, Count Roland, with death-defying mien.
Lo, at his side his comrade Oliver first is seen;
Thither came Gerin spurring, and now is Gerier there;
Otho is standing beside him; and lo, Duke Berenger,
Sansun the onset-leader, Anseïs the aweless-souled,
Ivon, Ivoire, whom their liege-lord dear to his heart doth hold:
Comes Engelier the Gascon, Girard of Roussillon
The agèd: of these Duke Gaifier the mighty maketh one.
And cried the Archbishop Turpin: "With thee will I go, by mine head!"
"Yea, I go with thee also," the good Count Walter said:
"Vassal I name me to Roland; it is meet that beside him I stand."
These chose knights twenty thousand to be of Roland's band.

66

Then Roland unto Walter his true man gave command:
"Take thou unto thee a thousand Franks of France our land;
Seize thou all mountain-gorges, all heights overhanging the path.
It beseems not that spoilers should pillage aught that the Emperor hath."
"For thee," made answer Walter, "will I do this faithfully."
He spurreth his steed, he waveth his sword uplifted high:
With a thousand Franks behind him he scours each ridge and height,
Nor thence is he thrust down plainward by all the clansmen's might,
Till out of their sheaths seven hundred swords have flashed in fight.
For Almaris the chieftain of the highlands of Balverne
On that day clashed with the hero in battle bitter and stern.

66 a

By this King Charles hath entered the Pass of Roncesvaux.
Before him leading the vanguard doth Ogier the war-duke go;
Yet on that side need for heedful guarding is little enow.
But Roland the while abideth on the side that looketh to Spain:
There Oliver beside him and the Twelve Peers all remain;
Mailed warriors twenty thousand, all Franks of France, there wait.

Battle shall they have surely—God help them in this strait!
But this that perjured traitor Ganelon only knows:
Gold is the price of his silence, and he keepeth the secret close.

67

High are the mountains, and gloomy the gorges; the black cliffs lower;
Grim are the passes where toileth with pain the Franks' war-power.
Folk fifteen leagues from the mountains heard their trampling's thunder.
But so soon as they won to the hill-crest, and beheld far-stretching thereunder
Gascony, land of their liege-lord, they remembered fief and domain,
Children, and noble ladies, and their tears burst forth like rain.
But Charles above all hath anguish, because at the gates of Spain
He hath left his nephew: from weeping for ruth he cannot refrain.

68

In Spain have the Twelve Peers tarried with the Franks of their war-array,
Twenty dreadless thousands; no fear of death know they.
But onward to France still fareth the Emperor weeping sore;
And he teareth his beard, his visage with his mantle he covereth o'er.
Now hard by his side was riding Naimes, and he asked of the King:
"For what hast thou heaviness?" "Cruel thou art to ask this thing!"
Said Charles: "I have so great sorrow that I cannot choose but lament;
For I know that by Ganelon's plotting shall France be ruin-rent.
Unto me in the night did a vision brought by an angel appear,
Wherein this Ganelon shivered within mine hands my spear.
It is he that hath doomed my nephew with the rearguard there to remain
In the alien marches, encompassed by the hoarded hate of Spain.
Ah God, if I lose him, never shall I see his like again!"

69

Charlemagne cannot refrain him from weeping, and all his array
Have ruth of him, and for Roland with a strange fear tremble they.
For Ganelon the felon hath fashioned treachery,
And costly gifts hath he taken from the King of Heathenry,
Jewels of gold and of silver, rich vesture and silken pall,
Fair mules and goodly horses, camels and lions withal.

Marsila the while hath summoned to a council his barons of Spain:
There is many a count and viscount and duke and warrior thane,
Many a dark-faced emir, and many an earldom's heir.
In three days' space four thousand of his lords hath he gathered there.
Through all Saragossa with thunder of tambours throbbeth the air.
They have hoisèd Mahomet's image to the height of their highest tower,
And the thronging paynims are praying unto that demon-power
To help them against Count Roland in battle's stormy hour.
Then gat they to horse, and forward they rode in furious haste.
Over the far-stretching lowland, o'er valley and hill have they passed;
And now they descry the banners of France as they flutter afar;
The ensigns of that rearguard, of the Twelve Companions, they are.
Ha! these not long shall tarry to clash in the shock of war!

70

Now cometh Marsila's nephew to the presence of the King:
The speed of his mule high-mettled with a staff is he hastening.
He uplifteth his voice and crieth to his uncle, laughing for glee:
"Long time have I rendered service, my fair lord, unto thee:
For thee have I borne much travail of war and manifold pain;
Victories many in battle for thee did my good sword gain.
For but one boon make I petition of thee, even Roland's head!
By the edge of my sword keen-shearing swiftly shall he be sped,
If the Prophet Mahomet vouchsafe me the glory thereof to gain;
And so will I deliver broad tracts of the land of Spain:
From the mountain-gates of Aspra to Durestant all shall be free:
Ay, Charles shall wax war-weary, and his Franks afar shall flee.
Then shalt thou rest from warfare so long as thou shalt live."
His prayer hath Marsila granted, his gauntlet for pledge doth he give.

71

Now doth Marsila's nephew in his hand that gauntlet hold,
And unto his uncle he crieth in accents proud and bold:
"Fair Sire, O King, thou hast given a gift of price untold!
Now then of thy mighty barons choose me eleven, that so
I may single out in the battle those Twelve Peers of the foe."

3—2

Then first of all those champions made answer Falsaron:
Blood-brother unto Marsila the King was that mighty one:
"Even I, fair sire my nephew, at thy right hand will go.
We twain in battle surely will close with yonder foe:
We twain upon the rearguard of Charles' great host will fall.
Now doomed are the Twelve Companions, appointed to death are they all!"

72

    Overagainst him riseth Corsabrin, the lord
Of Barbary, a serpent in act, ever false in word;
But now like a loyal vassal and knightly speaketh he:
"For all gold God hath created, craven I would not be!
If I come on this Roland, spare him I will not, but smite and slay.
Lo, I am the third of thine helpers; choose thee a fourth straightway."
But lo, Malprimès of Brigal is there in the hour of need;
More swiftly afoot he speedeth than one that rideth a steed.
Before Marsila he standeth, in a mighty voice doth he call:
"I also will bring this body to the fight at Roncesval.
If I light upon this Roland, I will leave him not till he fall!"

73

    An Emir of Balgherra mid the champions stood thereby;
His body was goodly-shapen, his glance was proud and high;
Mounted upon his war-horse, kingly his arms he bare,
A vassal worship-worthy, of courtesy debonair:
Had he been but a Christian, surely a right good knight had he been.
Now in presence of King Marsila he crieth with gallant mien:
"Unto Roncesval I also am fain this body to bear;
If I light upon Roland, an ending shall swift death make of him there,
Ay, and of Oliver also, and the Twelve Peers one and all:
In anguish and dishonour shall those Frank champions fall.
For Charles, he is now eld-stricken, and him need no man dread:
Soon shall he flinch from the war-toil; of him no host shall be led.
So Spain shall be left to her people in quiet possession for aye—
Ay, and we yet may win us the land of France for a prey!"
With manifold thanks did Marsila those heartening words repay.

74

Thereby stood an Almansor of the city Buriane—
Was no such felon paynim in all the land of Spain :—
Before Marsila he cometh, and loud he maketh his boast:
"Unto Roncesval I also will lead my warrior-host,
Vassals twenty thousand arrayed with lance and shield.
If I light upon Roland, assurance I give that to death he is sealed;
And Oliver and the Companions Twelve shall be overborne
By the pangs of death, and Frank-land shall sit of her children forlorn.
Not a day shall pass thereafter but Charles for the lost shall mourn."

75

Now rose Count Turgis, the ruler of Tortolosa, to speak—
Much evil upon the Christians, if he have but his will, shall he wreak ;—
And he joined himself to the champions in Marsila's presence arrayed ;
And he cried to the King: "In no wise be thou, O King, dismayed!
Mahound is more in puissance than Peter their saint of Rome!
Render him faithful service, and we lead thee in triumph home.
At Roncesval with Roland will I stand face to face:
Then, who shall give him assurance from death, when mine arm I raise?
Look on my sword—fine-tempered it is, and its blade is long:
With Durendal will I match it, the brand renowned in song;
Then, whether of twain is the better, ye shall see my steel decide.
Ay, all yon Franks shall perish, if they dare our coming abide;
And Charles the King, the dotard, shall have sorrow and shame enow:
The crown of lordship thereafter shall shine no more on his brow."

76

Then Escremiz of Valterna, a mighty man in his land,
Pressed through the throng, and shouting before the King did he stand:
"To Roncesval fare I, to humble the pride of the arrogant there!
If I light upon this Roland, his head no more shall he wear,
Neither shall Oliver, chiefest though he be of their array ;
For the Twelve Companions are sentenced to perish all in a day.
Yon Franks shall die, and for ever shall France be bereaved of her sons,
And Charles shall have sore anguish, forlorn of his mighty ones."

77

And thereby stood a paynim Esturganz, with his comrade Estramariz—
Evil companions, for traitors exceeding cunning were these.
Then spake unto these Marsila: "My lords, press on to the fray,
To Roncesval's mountain-gateway; there lead my war-array."
And they answered: "At thy commandment on Roland and Oliver,
Sire, we will fall: of a surety, death to the Twelve is near!
Behold our swords keen-whetted; the steel thereof is good:
As we swing them, they shall be crimson full soon with Christian blood.
The Franks shall perish, shall perish, and bitterly Charles shall grieve,
And to thee his great dominions as spoil of war will we give.
Thither, O King, betake thee! Doubt not, thou shalt take the prey.
We will make the Emperor yield him to thee in the triumphing day!"

78

Now Margariz of Sibilia hasteneth thitherward:
Even unto Camarías of the land was he overlord.
Of such gallant knightly bearing amidst the paynims was none;
Yea, the hearts of all fair ladies by his goodlihead were won.
Never a woman beheld him, but her face lit up at the sight;
Willed she or no, with smiling were her lips and her eyes alight.
Rang mid that press of champions his voice above the rest,
As he spake to the King: "For nothing dismayed, my lord, be thy breast!
I will go and slay this Roland at Roncesval in the strife;
Yea, Oliver from the battle shall not redeem his life;
And the Twelve Peers' blood shall be poured out as the blood of their martyrs was spilt.
Look upon this my war-glaive with its glorious golden hilt:
A gift unto me from the Emir of the city of Primes it came.
I pledge me to thee that crimsoned with their blood shall be this same.
Yon Franks shall perish, shall perish, and France shall be crushed with shame!
And as for Charles the dotard, with his beard of the winter snow,
Not a day shall pass, but his portion shall be self-reproach and woe.
Within one year shall we conquer France, at our feet shall she be.
We shall rest in the burg of Saint Denis in peace after victory."
To the vaunter Marsila bowed him lowly and gratefully.

79

Last, forth from the throng Chernuble the lord of Moneira stept.
By the mane of his locks dark-flowing the ground at his feet was swept.
When he trieth his strength, a burden yet greater can he upraise
Than seven strong mules which be laden for trampling the rugged ways.
In the land whence that count cometh, a dreary land forlorn,
Never the sun shines, never grows unto ripeness the corn;
Never the rain there falleth, nor ever droppeth the dew;
Nor a stone on the land's face lieth but is utterly black of hue:
Yea, the land is of devils haunted, as say folk not a few.
Spake this Chernuble: "Girded is my good sword unto my side,
And at. Roncesval as I swing it, shall its blade be crimson-dyed.
If on Roland I light, if encountered I be of this valorous lord,
Then, if I fall not upon him, let no man trust my word!
My sword, when the blades meet clashing, shall vanquish Durendal.
So France, when her best Franks perish, into utterest ruin shall fall."
Made up is the tale of the champions twelve with this last boast.
A hundred thousand vassals be arrayed in their battle-host.
Eager they are, yea, thirsting for the clash of the conflict they are;
And now 'neath a grove of fir-trees have they donned their harness of war.

80

All-armed are the Saracen warriors in shirts of the linkèd mail,
Link over link, even twofold, to be of the more avail.
Many a valiant paynim his helm on his head hath laced,
And his sword of the steel in Vienna forged hath he girt to his waist.
Fair glitter the shields, and the lances of Valentian steel flash bright,
And the pennons therefrom that flutter are scarlet and blue and white.
The mule is left in the meadow, the palfrey is not for the fray,
But on great war-horses mounted march they in serried array.
Fair was the morning, unclouded the sun was shining clear,
And his beams danced light on the ripples of that sea of battle-gear:
Blew up a thousand war-horns till the air laughed laughter of war;
That stern wide-rolling thunder have the Frank host heard from afar.

Cried Oliver: "Comrade, battle with the paynim is nigh, I trow!
Spake Roland the battle-eager: "God grant it may be so!
Good is it here for our master to endure whatsoe'er shall betide.
The vassal that fights for his liege-lord shall manifold travail abide:
He shall fear not for frost nor for snowdrift, nor for scorching heat shall he care:
He will give to the sword's devourings his very flesh and his hair.
Now deal great strokes and heavy, each man with his uttermost might!
Of us no song of dishonour shall be chanted by minstrel-wight!
The wrong is with yonder paynims, the right with the host of the Lord:
On glory's path will I lead them, unto honour shall point my sword."

81

To a high knoll Oliver spurreth, to the right he looketh therefrom:
Up the long green valley marching he seeth the Saracens come.
He calleth unto him Roland, and thus commune these twain:
"I see a great host marching hitherward from Spain:
There be flaming helms by thousands, and a sea of the bright mail-rings:
On, under his paynim rider, full many a fleet barb springs.
Bitter fury of battle awaiteth our little band.
This surely is Ganelon's doing! Lo, here is the traitor's hand!
By him thrust on was our liege-lord to doom us here to stand."
"Peace, Oliver!" swiftly and sternly Roland's answer came:
"The man at the least is my kinsman; I will hear no word to his shame."

82

From the height of the crest of the barrow o'er Spain looketh Oliver yet,
And the Saracen multitude seeth in array of battle set.
Helms gold-begemmed are flashing, shields blaze against the sun,
The mail-coats glint through the surcoats with broidery overdone;
As sway the lances, flutter and flash the pennons thereon.
There many a stately charger steps proudly beneath a knight:
Surges on surges of war-waves!—their numbers baffle sight;
Yea, Oliver's spirit is 'wildered, that he may not count them aright.
Down from the crest of the barrow full swiftly hath he spurred;
He hath come to the Frankish heroes, bearing an evil word.

83

"I have seen the paynim war-host," to his fellows Oliver cried;
"Never was huger beholden by men that on earth abide.
Ranked shields a hundred thousand of men-at-arms have I seen,
Seen laced on their heads their helmets, their mail all glittering sheen;
Strong dark-brown staves of lances, like a forest of pines, they bear:
High-borne on the long-maned horses steadily onward they fare.
Now shall ye have grim battle such as never did man behold.
God keep your ranks from flinching, O true hearts aweless-bold,
Lest haply by heathen foemen backward your lines should be rolled!"
And the Franks all shouted in answer: "A curse upon him who shall flee!
Lead thou: to the death we follow; no man shall be wanting to thee."

84

But again cried Oliver: "Mighty is the paynim host of war,
And passing few, meseemeth, the men of the rearguard are.
Sound Olifant, Roland my comrade: let the mighty horn peal out,
So Charles shall hear it, and straightway will he wheel his ranks about,
And he and all his army shall come to our aid straightway."
"Ay, and a fool's part," fiercely he answered, "should Roland play!
Throughout sweet France thenceforward of glory were I shorn,
If for any paynim living I should stoop to sound mine horn!
Ere then where blows are hailing shall Durendal's lightning gleam:
To the gold on the hilts that burneth with blood shall he reek and stream.
To their own destruction the felons have fared to the mountains' gate,
For, I swear by my faith and mine honour, they have rushed upon their fate."

85

"Sound Olifant, Roland my brother; so Charles shall hear it, and back
Will he turn, and will strike with his barons on our side in the battle-wrack."
"So please God," Roland answered, "never my kindred through me
Shall be brought to reproach, nor our country be stained with infamy!

Many a blow most mighty ere then shall Durendal deal,
He at my side that swingeth, the true and trenchant steel.
Thou shalt see red blood down-streaming from the point to the hilt of my brand.
For their ruin the felon paynims have gathered against our band,
For, I swear by my faith and mine honour, their death is hard at hand."

86

"Sound Olifant, Roland my comrade, and straightway shall Charlemagne hear:
He is threading the mountain-gorges still—O yet is he near.
Full soon, mine honour I pledge thee, will the banners of France appear."
"Now God forbid," cried Roland, "that for any heathen born
It shall ever be said that Roland hath stooped to sound his horn!
Shall I be on the lips of my kinsmen a byword, a shame, and a scorn?
No! in the mighty battle, in the heart of its tempest-roar,
Sword-strokes will I smite a thousand—ay, and seven hundred more!
Ye shall see Sword Durendal streaming and steaming with paynim gore.
The Franks, please God, like vassals shall battle, like knights without stain;
But none shall redeem from destruction the caitiff hordes of Spain."

86 *a*

"Once more I pray thee, O Roland my brother, sound thine horn!
To the Emperor Charles of Frankland so shall its voice be borne.
The warriors of France will swiftly return, by their thousands arrayed,
And into the alien country will bring unto us their aid."
"Now God the Father forbid it"—the words indignant ring—
"And Mary, our Lord's sweet Mother, that I should do this thing,
That I should sound this war-horn for any pagan host,
And that sunny France's glory through act of mine should be lost!
Now nay, I will smite on ever with Durendal my sword,
Till his very hilt be crimsoned with the blood that adown him hath poured.
To their own destruction hither the felon paynims came.
For me, it were better to perish than that France should be brought to shame!"

87

Spake Oliver: "Touching dishonour, none do I see therein;
For the countless Saracen war-host of the land of Spain have I seen.
The face of the lowland is hidden, the mountains are flooded o'er;
Over the stretches of moorland and down the valleys they pour.
Such a host be the alien people that past all telling be they,
And exceeding scant is the number of this our Frankish array.
Oh sound thine horn!—for the last time I ask it—and Charles shall hear!"
"Many are they?—the greater is my joy of the battle near!
God and his saints and angels forbid that France through me
Lose honour! Ere then shall my war-glaive hew full mightily.
Better it is that I perish than in shame drag out my life!
Now, for the love of our liege-lord, let us deal good blows in the strife."

88

Fearless is Roland, but prudence with valour joined doth remain
With Oliver: passing knightly is the courage of these twain.
They have armed them, have mounted their horses; now never more at all
Will they flinch from the shock of battle for fear lest death befall.
O yea, these earls be noble, and their words be proud and high:
But the heathen in fury riding by this have drawn full nigh.
"Turn thither thine eyes, O Roland," spake Oliver again:
"Mark—nigh to us now be the foemen, but afar is Charlemagne.
While yet there was help in the war-horn, to sound it thou wouldst not deign,
Else here even now were our liege-lord, and no hurt had we ta'en.
Now lift up thine eyes, gaze yonder toward Aspra's mountain-gate;
Thou canst see our rearguard, where sadly they look in the face of Fate:
Ay, many who never in rearguard again shall stand, there wait."
"Speak no such words!" cried Roland, "an offence unto me are they.
A curse upon him in whose bosom a heart beats faint with dismay!
We will bide the brunt of battle, we will yield no foot of ground;
Mighty shall be our sword-strokes, we will make this fight renowned."

89

Glowed Roland's face with the rapture of fight, as the foe drew nigh.
Like a lion he stood or a leopard with a proud stern light in his eye.
To the sons of France he shouted, and to Oliver he said:
"Dear friends, and noble companion, let us speak no whisper of dread!
The honour of France is committed to our hands by our King this day:
He hath set these twenty thousand apart from all his array:
He knoweth them all, and he knoweth that not one coward is there!
Manifold travail the vassal who fights for his lord shall bear:
He shall fear not for frost nor for snowdrift, nor for scorching heat shall he care;
And to him as dust in the balance shall be his flesh and his blood.
Strike with thy lance full knightly, as I with my war-glaive good,
With Durendal, who was given to me of the King my lord.
If I perish, who bears it hereafter shall speak thereof this word:
'Of a knight without stain, of a noble vassal, was this the sword.'"

90

Then Turpin the Archbishop to a knoll his war-horse spurred,
And the hearts of France's heroes with his battle-sermon he stirred:
"Lords barons, 'tis Charles, our liege-lord, who hath bidden us here to remain:
Lo you, it is our glad duty to die for our suzerain.
Ye stand here Christendom's champions; maintain her cause and her right!
Hereof have fullest assurance, that hard at hand is the fight:
Lift up your eyes, and behold them, the Saracens full in sight.
Kneel then, ye barons, confess you, and ask forgiveness of God:
I from your sins will absolve you, your souls shall cast their load;
Then, if haply ye fall in the battle, as holy martyrs ye die,
And for you be prepared God's mansions in his Paradise on high."
They dismounted, they knelt, and he blessed them in God's name; then cried he:
"Ye shall smite the infidel paynim, and your penance this shall be."

91

Then rose the Frankish warriors to their feet, absolved and shriven:
Cleansed from their sins, the Archbishop hath sealed them children of heaven.
Their swift war-steeds have they mounted; clad are they in manner meet

For knights: for the imminent battle are they armed from the head to the feet.
Unto Oliver spake Count Roland: "My friend and companion, I know
Full well whose false contriving hath doomed us unto the foe,
How Ganelon hath taken sin's hire of treasure and gold;
But for us shall the Emperor's vengeance fall on the treacherous-souled.
Of our lives this King Marsila foul merchandise hath made;
But our swords shall render him quittance, he shall to the full be repaid!"

92

Into the mountain-gateway of Spain doth Roland ride:
Upon Veillantif is he mounted, the steed of the long swift stride.
He rideth arrayed in his armour, in sooth a goodly sight!
His long lance lightly swaying that baron bears upright
With the steel head circling and flashing glints of flame to the sky:
Bound to the point doth a dove-white pennon flutter and fly,
And his hands are swept by its golden fringes swinging light.
Goodly and gallant he showeth, his face is smiling and bright;
And close behind him is riding the comrade of all most dear;
And the sons of France acclaim him their champion with cheer on cheer.
He looked on the Saracen foemen, and his glance was stern and high;
He looked on the Franks, his brethren, humbly and lovingly,
And with speech as of knight most courteous to these doth their captain cry:
"Lords barons, yet for a little the steed's impatience rein.
In quest of their own huge slaughter comes the heathen host of Spain:
But for us there is spoil of battle, a fair and goodly prey;
Frank King won never such costly booty unto this day."
As he ended, the fronts of battle were at point to close in the fray.

93

Then Oliver spake unto Roland: "The time for words is past.
Thou wouldst not deign on thy war-horn to sound the rescue-blast,
And the hope of Charlemagne's succour thou to the winds hast cast;
So then is he utterly blameless, for nothing hereof he knows,
And none may reproach his barons that they help not against our foes."
Then he cried to the Franks: "Lords barons, charge on the foe! Spur hard!

See that ye hold unflinching the gates ye were bidden to guard!
In the name of God I beseech you, resolve you to deal with the sword
Great blows, and receive them! Forget not the banner of Charles your lord!"
At his words from the Frankish war-host went up one shattering shout—
"Montjoy!"—whosoever hath heard it, when that war-cry rings out,
He is thrilled with the spirit of valour, he thinketh of nought beside.
Then did they charge—in what scorning of death, Great God, did they ride!
Hard spurred they: the racing chargers too slowly, they thought, on-dashed:
Then—ha, what else would ye look for?—down on the foemen they crashed.
Yea, and with hearts unflinching the foe their onset await;
And the armies are locked in the wrestle of a battle grim and great.

94

Now a nephew there was of Marsila, and Aelroth he had to name:
From the host of the paynim foremost spurring forth he came,
And against our Franks he shouted defiance with words of shame:
"Ha, felon Franks, ye shall meet us now in the deadly joust!
Lo, he who should have defended you hath betrayed your trust!
Mad was your King, at the mountain-gate to leave you forlorn,
Whereby sweet France of her glory shall soon be utterly shorn,
Yea, and from Charlemagne's body shall his right arm be torn."
When Roland heard that vaunting, to anguish of wrath was he stirred:
In fury he rode against him, his charger to speed hath he spurred.
To wreak on the count his vengeance each sinew doth he strain;
He bursteth through his buckler, he cleaveth his hauberk in twain;
The shock of the great spear pierceth the midst of his body through;
Clear through his breast it leapeth, the bones are riven in two:
Onward the point rushed, rending the very spine from its place,
And out through that red gateway his soul doth the lance-head chase.
Rocked and reeled the body before that thunderbolt-thrust;
From the saddle the spear hath lifted and hurled him down to the dust.
So heavily fell he earthward that his neck in sunder burst.
Even now could not Roland refrain him, but that dead railer he cursed:
"Out on thee, caitiff!" he shouted, "no fool is Charles our lord,
And treason to friend or to foeman for ever his soul hath abhorred!

Right nobly he did, that he left us to guard the pass this day:
No leaf from the crown of glory of France shall fall away.
Strike, sons of France! The omen is ours of the first death-blow.
The right is with us, the true men, the wrong with the treacherous foe!

95

In the paynim host was a war-lord, and Falsaron his name,
Which was brother to King Marsila: from the realm accursed he came
Where Dathan and Abiram alive went down into hell.
'Neath the firmament's arch no felon abode more fierce and fell.
Betwixt his eyes so monstrous was the span of his demon-face
That scarce in half a foot-breadth might ye measure out the space.
In anguish of wrath, beholding where dead his nephew lay,
He burst through the press, and he showed him in the forefront of the fray;
He cried the paynim war-cry, he charged in fury down
On the Franks: "This day," he shouted, "shall sweet France lose her renown!"
Oliver heard it; in anger he pricked with the spurs of gold
His charger, and rode to smite him like baron knightly-souled.
His lance hath burst through his buckler, through the hauberk the steel hath gone,
And deep in his body are buried the laps of the gonfalon.
Over the arch of the saddle the shaft hath lifted the dead,
And down on the earth hath dashed him: so is a traitor sped!
O'er him the conqueror shouteth with scornful triumph-cry:
' For thy threatening vaunts, thou caitiff, little enow care I!
Strike, sons of France! Full lightly shall we conquer the heathen rout!
Montjoy!" he cried, far-pealing King Charles's victory-shout.

96

Came forth from their host a champion, the King of Barbary,
Corsabrin, lord of a country afar off oversea;
And to all his Saracen vassals vauntingly cried their King:
"But little toil or travail this battle to us shall bring.
Behold yon Frank battalions, how thin the ranks of them are!
Little enow need we tremble before their prowess in war!
Ha, long shall they bide unholpen ere Charles their King draw nigh!'

This is the day of their dooming: themselves but look to die!"
But Turpin the lord Archbishop that vaunter's defiance hath heard,
And by no man under the heavens unto grimmer wrath was he stirred.
Into the flanks of his charger he hath driven his spurs of gold:
Onward to smite him he raceth, that baron knightly-souled.
He hath burst through his buckler, the hauberk-links asunder spring,
And deep in the felon's body his lance is quivering.
At the thunderbolt-shock of his onset did the body reel and sway;
From the saddle the spear hath lifted and dashed him down in the way.
He looked on the fallen traitor, dead on the earth as he lay,
Nor now can Turpin refrain him from shouting the triumph-cry:
"Out on thee, caitiff and dastard! Lo there thine hire for thy lie!
King Charles our lord will be surety for us to the uttermost.
No thought have they of fleeing, the men of our Frankish host!
We will see to it that thy comrades shall not go hence with life:
They have never known such slaughter as awaits them in this day's strife.
Strike, strike, ye Franks! Forget not that ye come of noble strain!
Thank God, we have drawn the first blood! With us doth the vantage remain!
Montjoy! Montjoy!" he shouted, that the whole field rang again.

97

Now dashed to the earth by Gerin is Malprimès the lord of Brigal.
Of none avail is his buckler, for shattered in sunder fall
The halves of the boss of crystal in the centre thereof: he hath torn
From his body his hauberk, and earthward impaled on the lance is he borne.
Out of life into death swift-stricken in the dust doth the paynim roll,
And Satan straightway cometh, and hellward beareth his soul.

98

Now Gerier, comrade of Gerin, hath hurled the Emir to the dust:
Shattered his shield is, his hauberk-links are rent by the thrust,
And the long lance deep in his entrails hath buried its fierce steel tip.
Out of the saddle he heaved him with the lance in his giant grip,
And down to the earth he dashed him. And Oliver marked it, and cried:
"Ha, in full knightly fashion the heroes strike on our side!"

99

Now rideth forth Duke Sansun to fight with the Almansor:
His shield hath he shattered, emblazoned with gold and with flowers all o'er,
And the linkèd mail of his hauberk fenceth his life in vain,
For his heart, his lungs, and his liver the spear-head teareth in twain.
Grieve who will for the stricken, death with the stroke hath gone;
And the Archbishop cried: "A knightly stroke! Right well hast thou done."

100

Then did the lord Anseïs set spurs to his battle-steed:
Upon Turgis of Tortolosa he swoopeth with eagle-speed.
Above the boss gold-gleaming is the shield by the lance pierced through:
The doublets of his hauberk by the shock are rent in two.
Deep into the vaunter's body hath plunged the point of the spear;
So stark was the stroke that the lance-head behind him stood out clear:
With a mighty heave of the spear-shaft is he hurled from the selle to the grass.
"The stroke of a knightly vassal," cried Roland, "in sooth that was!"

101

Then Engelier of Burdel, the gallant Gascon knight,
Set spurs to the flanks of his charger, and with loosened rein forthright
With Escremiz of Valterna in hurricane onset he clashed.
The shield from his neck hath he smitten, and all to shards hath dashed:
The hauberk-rings are rifted, the neck-piece torn away:
Above his breast doth the lance-point light, and it makes no stay,
But impaled on the shaft from the saddle is he hurled, struck dead at a blow.
Over him shouted the victor: "Thou wast doomed unto death long ago!"

102

Otho against Esturganz chargeth across the field,
And his lightning spear-point rendeth the covering of his shield:
The crimson overbroidered on the white asunder is shorn,
And the doublets from his mail-coat by the ruthless steel are torn.
The ashen shaft hath impaled him, the red point stands out clear:
Down from the saddle he hurleth him dead, and with triumph-jeer
He shouted: "Ha, small surety for your lives shall ye find here!"

W. C. R. 4

103

On Estramariz now rideth Berenger the noble peer:
He hath dashed his shield in pieces, hath rifted his mail with the spear.
Clear through the paynim's body the unswerving steel hath sped:
Mid Saracens slain a thousand, to earth has he fallen dead.
So now, of the heathen champions twelve, ten peers lie slain,
Yea, there abide yet living of all which vaunted in vain
Count Margariz one, and Chernuble the other: there be but twain.

104

A knight of exceeding prowess is the paynim Margariz;
Comely to look on and stalwart, lithe and swift he is.
He spurreth his steed, he singleth Oliver out in the fray:
Through the golden boss of his buckler the spear-point cleaveth its way;
Unto Oliver's side the lance-head came exceeding nigh,
But the hand of God preserved him, and his flesh was ungashed thereby,
Though cold o'er his skin as the finger of death slid the steel of the spear.
On rode the heathen, as finding nought to stay his career,
And to summon around him his vassals his horn pealed loud and clear.

105

A mad mellay is the battle by this, a tempest of strife:
Through the heart of it storms Count Roland, reckless wholly of life.
With his lightning lance he thrusteth, so long as endureth the shaft,
Till the fifteenth blow hath shivered and splintered it down to the haft.
From the scabbard, like flame out of darkness, the good sword Durendal flashed.
He spurred the flanks of his war-horse, and down on Chernuble he dashed:
He smote on the crest of his helmet, where blazing a ruby shone:
Through head and through hair keen-cleaving the trenchant blade hath gone;
The brow 'twixt the eyes is sundered, and all the visage therewith.
Cleft are the links of the hauberk, the cunning work of the smith:
The fierce edge severs the body in twain from the throat to the waist:
It sheareth through the saddle with bands of gold overbraced;
Yea, into the war-horse plungeth the steel of the battle-glaive keen;

Through the backbone it biteth, nor searcheth a space the bones between.
So flung are the horse and the rider dead on the thick greensward:
"Base churl!" he cried, "to thy sorrow thou camest hitherward!
No whit of thy prophet Mahomet shalt thou be holpen now,
Nor won shall be any battle by such vile caitiffs as thou!"

106

This way and that way rideth Count Roland across the field:
Durendal, mighty to sever and to pierce, doth his strong hand wield:
Huge was the havoc of paynims that marked his path as he sped.
Ha, to have seen him hurling one on another dead!
To have seen the earth around him with blood and with brains bespread!
All ruddy-streaked was his hauberk, from his sword-arm dripped the blood:
From his charger's neck and shoulders streamed the crimson flood.
And Oliver rode anear him: not slow was his hand to smite!
Of the Twelve was none but bare him as an utter-blameless knight.
The Franks are pressing behind them, and ever they smite and slay.
Here slain outright fell paynims, and there in the death-swoon lay.
"Well do they ward them, our barons!" the stout Archbishop cried:
"Now God vouchsafe that our liege-lord have many such beside!"

107

On rode Oliver, breasting the battle's tempest-roar:
Shivered his lance was, the truncheon alone in his hands he bore;
Yet Malsaron the paynim with that war-mace did he smite.
Therewith did he shatter his helmet with gold and with flowers bedight.
So stark was the blow, from his forehead his eyeballs were dashed to the ground,
And his very brains were scattered at his feet on the earth around.
So he hurled him amidst seven hundred slaughtered heathen to lie.
Then Turgin and Esturguz met him, and met him to die.
But the last blow splintered the truncheon; to the haft is it shattered now.
Then cried down the war-wind Roland: "My comrade, what doest thou?
In such a battle of giants for staves is there no place!
Here steel of the sword shall avail us alone, or the iron mace.
Where is the sword far-famous?—doth Haltclere hide from the fight,

4—2

The brand with the hilts all-golden, with the pommel of diamond bright?"
"No time have I had to draw it," Oliver cried unto him,
" For my need of ceaseless smiting was so exceeding grim!"

108

From the sheath hath Oliver plucked it, even as his comrade bade,
And he flashed in the eyes of Roland in knightly wise that blade;
And Justin of Valferra of the paynims first must feel
Its edge, for wholly asunder his head was cleft by the steel;
It flashed through the helm, through the hauberk with broidery overlaid;
All down the length of his body it held its course unstayed;
The fang of steel hath bitten clear through the gilded selle,
And the charger's spine is severed by the stroke so fierce and fell;
Down dashed he warrior and war-horse dead at his feet on the mead;
Roland marked it, and shouted : "Now know I my brother indeed!
For battle-strokes so mighty our Emperor holdeth us dear!"
And from every hand the war-cry "Montjoy!" pealed loud and clear.

109

Lo, cometh Count Gerin bestriding Sorel his battle-steed,
With Gerier his friend, whose charger outstrippeth the wild hart's speed.
With loose reins both are they spurring against the infidel,
And side by side come charging on the paynim Timozel.
Their lances have crossed in his body through hauberk and through shield:
Dead is he cast mid the furrows of death's grim harvest-field.
By whose hand first was he smitten?—I know not : no bard saith
From which of the twain came flashing first the lightning of death.
Mid the foe rode Espervaris, the son of the lord Borèl :
By the hand of the knight of Burdel, Engelier, he fell.
And there hath the stout Archbishop struck down Siglorel
The sorcerer, who descended once on a time into hell,
By Jupiter led thither through the power of the Evil One.
Cried Turpin : "One more felon the course of death hath run!"
And Roland answered : "The caitiff is vanquished verily!
O Oliver my brother, such good strokes gladden me!"

110

Now passing stern and bitter waxeth the battle-strain:
From the hands of Frank and heathen marvellous sword-strokes rain,
And here one wardeth the death-blow, and there one smiteth amain.
Many and many a spear-shaft might ye see with blood that dripped,
Many a pennon and banner to fluttering fragments ripped;
Many a gallant Frenchman shall there leave youth and life;
They shall look no more on a mother, nor see the face of a wife,
Nor their friends at the gates of the mountains who await their return from the strife.
And Charles the while is weeping afar, is sorrow-distraught—
But now what boots his repentance? His help can avail them nought!
Right evil service was done him of Ganelon, in that day
When he bartered in Saragossa the lives of his kindred away!
Ha, so did he thrust to destruction himself, both life and limb,
For at Aix was he doomed thereafter to a scaffold passing grim.
Yea, down did he drag in his ruin thirty kinsmen withal,
Who had thought not that death was his guerdon, nor looked by his treason to fall.

111

Now waxeth the battle wondrous, and its travail passing sore:
Well Oliver and Roland the burden of that day bore;
There the Archbishop fighteth, and a thousand sword-strokes ring;
There are the Twelve Peers smiting unflinching, unfaltering;
There are the Frank knights charging, as one man strike they all;
There are the paynims dying, by hundreds and thousands they fall.
Who turned not to flight, no surety he had from the imminent death:
Will he or no, there gaspeth he forth his latest breath.
But the Franks the while are losing their trustiest battle-gear:
Snaps many a lance-shaft, broken is the steel of many a spear:
Shattered in glittering fragments is the blade of many a sword:
Rolled red surges of battle over many a valiant lord
Who shall never behold a father nor a kinsman any more,
Nor his King, who in vain awaits him far off by the mountain-door.
But France the while with the turmoil of a marvellous tempest is loud:

There is storm with crashing thunder and wind: from bursting cloud
Cataract rains are pouring, measureless scourging of hail;
Thick and fast descendeth the thunderbolt's flashing flail;
And the very land's foundations with earthquake shiver and sway.
From St Michael du Peril to Xanten, from Besançon to Wissant Bay,
No dwelling there was but rifted were the walls thereof that day.
At noon was there utter darkness; if the heaven were not cloven apart,
No light shone: never a mortal but trembled with sinking heart.
Many a voice was crying: "This is the Day of Doom!
Now upon us of a surety the End of the World is come!"
Ah, but the truth they knew not; was none that boded aright:
That was the mourning of Nature for the Death of Roland the Knight!

III*a*

Wondrous great are the portents, and the tempest terrible:
Through France full many an omen evil-boding befell.
In the land from the height of noontide unto the vesper-hour
Is a night of palpable darkness; so heavy the thick clouds lower,
No light there is from the shining of the sun, no moon is there;
No man there is, but he looketh for death in his utter despair.
Well might there be such dolour in France, that day of all,
When that great battle-captain of a nation's strength must fall!
At St Denis it standeth recorded in the ancient minstrel's scroll
That in truth for the death of Roland creation mourned in dole.
Ah, there was none could surpass him, of all men on earth that dwell,
In conquering lands for his master, in smiting the infidel!
There was none that in tourney or battle could cast him from the selle.

III*b*

Now passing stern and bitter waxeth the battle-strain.
There with their swords' keen edges the Franks are hewing amain.
Yea, there was none whose falchion streamed not with heathen gore:
Aye rang the far-famed war-cry "Montjoy!" through the tempest-roar.
Lo, mid the paynim is panic, they flee through all the plain,
And the Franks pursue hard after, and no man draweth rein.

III c

Ha, ware·are they now, these paynims, how grim is the grapple of war!
From the stricken field are they streaming, fast fleeing, fleeing far!
"Take no man alive!" the avengers shout with relentless breath.
Lo, how the plains are covered with the swaths of the harvest of death!
Lo Saracens lying by thousands heaped on the grass splashed red,
While the burnished hauberks and mail-coats gleam on the breasts of the dead
Mid many a splintered spear-shaft and tattered gonfalon.
And lo, this first of the battles the heroes of France have won!
Ah God, what evils await them, what travail of battle-strain!
Ah, in what measureless sorrow shall France mourn over her slain!

112

The sons of our France have battled with courage proud and high:
Heaps upon heaps the paynims dead by their thousands lie.
Not two of a hundred thousand alive from the red field fly.
Then cried the Archbishop: "Our warriors right gallantly have striven!
No king hath better vassals 'neath the canopy of heaven!"
Yea, in our France's annals the record stands enscrolled
What men were the Emperor's vassals, how loyal and aweless-bold.
They passed o'er the field of battle, they sought their belovèd dead
The while for ruth and for sorrow tears from their eyes they shed
In anguish of love heart-broken for friends and kindred lost:
—Like a surging sea rolls nearer the while Marsila's host.

112 a

In very truth Count Roland is a passing stalwart knight.
Oliver and the Twelve Companions have borne them well in fight.
Not a Frank there is but hath stricken many a knightly blow:
Slain by their mighty prowess lies many a paynim foe.
Yea, of a hundred thousand there hath escaped but one,
Even Margariz—for his fleeing may he have blame of none!
Many a deep-scarred token of battle his body bore;
Pierced is his flesh through his armour by the steel of lances four;
So unto flight hath he turned him, and Spainward hasteneth,
And is come to Marsila, and telleth his tale of the havoc of death.

112 *b*

So there Count Margariz standeth, alone escaped from the field
With the butt of a broken spear-shaft, a shard of a shattered shield;
For round the boss of his buckler but half a foot doth remain;
His helmet is dinted and cloven, and hewn are its bands in twain;
Gashed is the mail of his hauberk, and link from link is rent,
And from hilt to point is his war-glaive with gouts of blood besprent;
Pierced is his flesh through his armour by the steel of lances four,
For he comes from a field of battle where blows were many and sore.
Ah, had he been but a Christian, what a knightly vassal he were!
Now unto King Marsila all things doth he declare.
In a great voice clear-ringing to his lord he straightway cried:
"Up, noble King of Espagna, to the battle swiftly ride!
Yon Franks of France forwearied with slaying the men of our host
Shalt thou find, and with ceaseless smiting: their shields and spears be lost,
Yea, lost be the half of their warriors, and more; and they that remain
Be feeble indeed, sore wounded, and dashed with crimson stain.
Scarce have they weapons to ward them: easy to vanquish be they!
Swiftly pursue them, and surely this is the vengeance-day!"
Leapt to their feet the paynims at his words, athirst for the fray.
From far have the Franks beheld them—on Roland and Oliver now
From the skirts of the field are they crying: "Sir Roland, where art thou?
Hither, O Twelve Companions, come, and strike on our side!"
First was the Archbishop to answer, and heartening them he cried:
"Vassals of God, acquit you like men! Be dauntless-souled!
This day on your brows in heaven shall God set crowns of gold,
And ye shall inherit mansions in His glorious Paradise."
Then doth a passion of sorrow and ruth through the host arise:
Of love for the dead and the doomed ones the tears flow fast from their eyes.
Now kiss they each the other with the kiss of charity.
"Ye barons, to horse!" far-ringing doth the voice of Roland cry:
"With knights a hundred thousand Marsila draweth nigh!"

113

Through the midst of a valley Marsila marcheth: his gathered array
In twenty mighty squadrons is ordered for the fray.
Flash gems and gold from the helmets, flutter the pennons bound
To the lances, gleam the bucklers and the mail-coats broidered round.
Sounding the battle-onset seven thousand trumpets blare;
Loud over the land far-wafted their thunder thrills the air.
Unto Oliver turneth Roland: "Companion and friend," he saith,
"All too truly and plainly hath Ganelon plotted our death.
No cloak for the sin remaineth, too clear the treason is.
Exceeding terrible vengeance will the Emperor take for this.
Hard at hand is battle, a battle bitter and stern:
Never hath mortal witnessed such flame of combat burn.
I will smite the ranks of the paynim with Durendal my brand,
And thou, my companion, with Haltclere smite: through many a land
Have we borne them, and many a battle with these have we won for our King.
Of us no song of derision shall minstrel ever sing!"

114

When now the Franks saw plainly how huge was the host of the foe,
How all the plain was covered with its surging overflow,
On Oliver and Roland full many voices cried,
And on the Twelve Peers many: "Good knights, stand fast on our side!"
First answering spake the Archbishop, Turpin the unafraid:
"O gallant knights, in no wise be any man dismayed!
In God's name I beseech you that ye think no thought of flight.
Of us no song of scoffing be sung by minstrel wight!
Better it were, far better, that all we died in the fight!
One thing to us all is promised, that here the end shall be:
Beyond this day no morrow on earth shall any see.
But for one thing am I surety unto you the absolved and shriven—
For you are prepared God's mansions in the Paradise of Heaven:
There amid saints and angels shall thrones unto you be given."
Then the ranks of France took courage from his words: their hearts beat high.
Then spurred the swift steeds forward that flower of chivalry—
"Montjoy! Montjoy!" they shouted; not a voice but swelled the cry.

114 *a*

Now of all kings this Marsila is the prince of treachery.
He saith to his paynim barons: "My lords, of a truth know ye
That Roland is passing valiant, of wondrous prowess in fight.
Who thinketh to overcome him must strive with his uttermost might.
Two battles, I trow, shall suffice not to quell this champion grim;
Three times must we hold us ready in combat to close with him.
This day shall Charles the haughty be stripped of the pride of his fame;
This day shall ye see France humbled in infamy of shame!
Now therefore, of twenty squadrons, with me shall ten abide,
And the other ten to the battle with the sons of France shall ride."
Then a banner with gold fringe broidered he gave unto Grandoine's hand,
That he against the Frenchmen might lead the first war-band;
So he took upon him the fulfilment of his lord the King's command.

114 *b*

On a hill Marsila remaineth to watch the fight from afar,
But onward Grandoine marcheth with all his men of war.
Across the valley riding in fiery haste hath he gone,
And with three gold clasps hath he fastened to his spear his gonfalon.
With a great voice then he shouted: "Ride on, ye barons all!"
Pealed out a thousand war-horns their loudest battle-call.
But the Franks cried: "God our Father, unto us what now shall befall?
In an evil day we beheld him, the traitor Ganelon, first!
He hath sold us unto the heathen with treachery accurst!
Now, O ye Twelve Companions, strike for our help on our side!"
First the Archbishop answered, and heartening them he cried:
"O gallant knights, high honour shall ye receive this day,
For crowns our God shall give you and flowers that fade not away
In Paradise His garden, amidst His glorified,
Through the gates whereof unto cowards is entrance ever denied."
"We will smite them shoulder to shoulder!" they shouted as with one breath:
"Never will we be traitors to France for dread of death!"
The golden spurs are striking, they are charging with loosened rein,
Charging down to the smiting of the felon hordes of Spain.
"Montjoy for Charles!" they shouted, till the whole field rang again.

114*c*

So King Marsila hath parted that second host in twain,
And hath chosen thereof ten squadrons still at his side to remain;
And ten are riding onward to clash in the shock of war.
A thousand trumpets are sounding, the blare is heard from afar.
"Ah God!" the Franks are crying, "for this our bitter strait!
Ah for the Twelve Peers tangled in the closing net of fate!"
Cheering their fainting spirits Archbishop Turpin cried:
"Good knights, our God of a surety fighteth upon your side.
This day with the fadeless flowers of Eden shall ye be crowned;
Thrones in the upper Heavens for you the war-renowned
In Paradise wait, where coward never hath entrance found."
Then leapt their hearts, and answered the Franks: "We will fail you not!
God helping us, our honour shall abide without one spot!
We will grapple with yon foemen unto our latest breath.
Few may we be, but within us is courage strong as death!"
Their steeds, as they shout, are they spurring to clash with the paynim-array—
Lo, Frank and Saracen mingled in the turmoil of the fray!

115

Now a paynim of Saragossa was in Grandoine's host that day,
And the half of all that city he held beneath his sway;
But the soul of a churl and a felon was in Climborin's mighty frame:
He had taken of Ganelon surety for doing the deed of shame,
For that betrayal of Roland and all his company:
On the lips had he kissed the traitor in token of amity,
And had given to him that helmet whereon did a ruby flame.
An oath, he said, had he taken to bring wide France to shame,
And to pluck the crown of lordship from the brows of Charles our King.
With fiery feet is his war-horse, Barbamusche, thundering—
A swifter steed than a falcon, fleeter than swallow's wing:—
Hard he spurreth him onward, on his neck the loose reins lie:
Upon Engelier is he charging, the lord of Gascony.
Nor shield nor corslet availeth that battle-weary peer;
Through armour and through body hath pierced the heathen spear.

So stark was the thrust, that behind him stood out the lance's head:
Borne on the long shaft earthward that noble knight fell dead.
Shouted the victor: "Foemen be these that 'tis good to slay!
Strike, strike, ye paynims! shatter their ranks in disarray!"
"Ah God!" cried the Franks, "what a hero is lost unto us this day!"

116

But marked was his fall of Roland; to Oliver cried he, and said:
"Behold now, O my companion, Count Engelier is dead—
He than whom none was braver, a knight without a stain!"
"Now God grant," Oliver shouted, "that I may avenge the slain!"
He hath smitten the flanks of his war-horse with golden spur on heel:
Haltclere on high is he swinging; the red blood drips from the steel.
He chargeth down on the paynim in the fulness of his might;
One shattering blow on his helmet, where cross the bars, doth he smite.
From brow unto chin with the headpiece the head is cloven in twain:
Sheer down through his body it biteth, and the very steed is slain.
As upswung in the hand of the slayer the blade, that Saracen fell,
And devils plucked from the body his soul, and bare it to hell.
Charged Oliver then on Alphayen the Duke, and with one blow slew;
He turned upon Escabábi, and hewed his head in two:
Seven Arabian captains from saddle to earth he bore—
No man of them all unto battle shall rise up any more!
Then Roland cried: "The anger of my comrade is passing grim.
Woe unto any foeman who dares to encounter him!
Deeds noble and worship-worthy he doeth by my side:
For such blows doth the Emperor love us, for so is he glorified.
Montjoy! Montjoy!" he shouted: "Strike hard, good knights!" he cried.

117

Now there rode mid the ranks of the paynim a felon more evil-souled
Than any in Spain: when Marsila the boy mid the knights was enrolled,
This Valdabrun was his sponsor, and buckled his spurs of gold.
He is lord of four hundred dromonds that plough for gain the sea;
Not a sailor there is but sweareth unto this man fealty.
Erewhile by craft of treason Jerusalem had he won,

Had polluted with foul defilement the temple of Solomon,
And the Patriarch had he murdered by the font's most holy stone.
Unto him had Ganelon given his pledge of treason: the sword
Priced at a thousand mangons had he given to that false lord.
Forth now he cometh bestriding Grandamunt his steed,
In whose feet is the storm-wind, swifter than a falcon's wing they speed.
He is spurring him on, he is couching at Sansun the Duke his lance—
Wide lordships he had and goodly in the pleasant land of France—
He hath shattered his buckler, the lance-head through his rifted hauberk hath gone:
Deep in his body are buried the laps of its gonfalon.
From the saddle heaved by the spear-shaft, on the sand the dead lieth low.
Shouted the victor: "Varlets! ye shall all die even so!
For Charlemagne's help be ye waiting?—he shall bring you little enow!
Strike, strike, ye paynims! Lightly shall we shatter their array!"
"Ah God!" cried the Franks, "what a hero is lost unto us this day!"

118

When Roland beheld how Sansun dead to the earth was thrown,
Grieved was he beyond all grieving that ever man hath known.
He setteth spurs to his war-horse, he raceth eager-souled,
In his hand Sword Durendal—precious was that above all fine gold!
He hath swooped on the paynim, with fury upgathered he smiteth hard:
The lightning blade down-flasheth on the helmet gold-bestarred.
It cleft through the head and the corslet; down through his body it shore;
It bit through the goodly saddle with gold bespangled o'er,
And deep in the back of his charger the steel its onrush stays.
That stroke slew horse and rider—let who will blame it or praise!
"Oh ruinous stroke!" the heathen cried in sore amaze.
Made answer Roland: "Hated of me evermore shall ye be!
Yours, proud and haughty scorners, is the wrong and the treachery!"

119

From Afric a Moorish warrior, Malquidant, had sailed,
King Malcud's son; in armour of beaten gold was he mailed:
Brighter than all other it flashed against the sun.

Bestriding his steed Salperdut—and swifter beast was none—
Sharply the spurs he driveth into his charger's side;
Against Anseïs' buckler couching his spear doth he ride.
The shield by the shock is shattered: its plates asunder fly;
The lappets of the hauberk are wrenched away thereby.
Clear through his body the lance-head, and the shaft of the lance, have passed,
And the slain, impaled on the spear-shaft, down on the earth is cast.
Dead is the Count Anseïs, the days of his life are fled;
And the Franks cried: "Noble baron, alas for thee, thou art sped!"

120

Through the press did Archbishop Turpin fiercely spurring pass—
Never of priest so noble was chanted holy mass!
Never was priest that accomplished such deeds of prowess as he!
At the paynim rode he, shouting: "God's malison on thee!
Mine heart for him thou hast stricken is wrung with bitter pain!
Now liever would I perish if I may not avenge the slain!
Down on the paynim chargeth the steed by the spurred heel stung:
Full on the shield in Toledo forged hath the spear-head rung:
Dead in the midst of his triumph on the green grass down is he flung.

121

Far thence mid the rolling battle the paynim Grandoine warred,
King Capuel's seed, the scion of Cappadocia's lord,
High-borne upon his war-horse, the good steed Marmorie hight,
Whose stormy feet were fleeter than the wings of a wild bird's flight.
The flanks of the barb he spurreth, he rideth on loose-reined:
Down upon Gerin he chargeth with thews to the thrust hard-strained.
Crashed on the crimson buckler the lance: the point hath gone
Clear through, and rending the hauberk the ruthless steel held on,
Till deep in his body buried was the spear-head's pennon blue.
Down on a rock up-jutting the hero's corse he threw:
Swiftly upon his companion Gerier he turned, and slew:
Berenger now hath he smitten, and Guy, St Antony's lord:
Against Count Austorie lightens now the unglutted sword—

The wealthy holder of Valence and the lordships that fringe the Rhone.
He hath slain him: exulted the paynims for all these overthrown.
"How fast are our noblest falling!" in anguish the Frenchmen groan.

122

Count Roland's hand is grasping a sword that with blood streams red—
Great God, on missions how many of death this day hath it sped!
To his ear is wafted the sorrow of the Franks that bewail their slain:
His heart with the sudden anguish is like to burst in twain.
On the paynim charged he, shouting: "God's curse upon thee for aye!
Good men and true hast thou murdered for whom thou dearly shalt pay!"
Forward the good steed leapeth at the touch of the spur in his side:
And face to face are the champions—with God must the issue abide.

123

Now this Grandoine was valiant and great in bodily might,
A vassal of prowess exceeding who never had flinched from fight.
But now stands Roland barring the path of the infidel:
Never had Grandoine seen him, yet knoweth him all too well
By the pride of the hero's visage, by the flashing eyes and keen,
By the goodlihead of his body, by the majesty of his mien.
He seeth a blade blood-streaming, he knoweth Durendal here!
In his heart's despite a panic hath seized him of deadly fear.
Fain would he flee the avenger, but nought it avails him now,
For the lightning of Roland's sword-stroke is flashing through his brow,
Hath hewn the helmet asunder, hath shorn the nose-piece in two:
His head from the crown hath it cloven down to the teeth clear through:
The body from throat to haunches, the hauberk's mail it divides;
It shears through the golden saddle with its silver-gleaming sides:
Into the back of the war-horse deep hath it bitten withal.
Dead on the field with his rider doth the sundered charger fall.
The Saracens saw that vengeance with a wail of grief and affright;
But the Franks cried: "Ha, right nobly doth our protector smite!"

124

Now is the battle wondrous, a rushing storm of fight:
The Franks are stabbing and lashing with sword-blades burnished bright:
They hew through thrusting spear-shafts, through targes flower-bescrolled;
They cleave the ringing helmets and their flaming bands of gold:
They give not one foot backward in fury of battle-strain.
Ah God, to see them slashing men's heads by scores in twain!
To see the hauberks rifted, the mail asunder shorn,
And the living flesh red-streaming through vesture shredded and torn!
Through the ranks of Spain such havoc, such ruin of death they bore,
That the green grass wholly was hidden by crimson pools of gore.
Then a wail went up from the paynims: "We can endure no more!
O land of France, of Mahomet be thou for ever accurst,
For, of all earth's children, in valour this people of thine be first!"
And with one voice now are they crying upon Marsila their King:
"Ride, ride, O gracious master, ride for our succouring!"

125

Now is the battle wondrous and waxen passing great.
The felon paynims are smiting in the rage of desperate hate;
And ever the Franks unsparing are slaying ruthlessly.
Measureless human anguish there thou mightest see.
By thousands dead, or wounded and bleeding to death, they lie
Heaped one on another, their faces earthward or turned to the sky:
Here, there, were good steeds many fleeing athwart the plain
Between their fore-feet trailing and tossing the masterless rein.
Now the Saracen host may no longer endure; the rent ranks yield:
Will they or no, they are breaking, are streaming back from the field.
Follow the Franks hard after, fiercely they hold in chase
Those fleers unto the borders of Marsila's camping-place.

125 *a*

First in pursuit is Roland, he smites like a stalwart knight:
The Franks on their swift war-horses press on the paynims' flight,

While the huddled foemen cumber each other the while they fly:
As they press through the hollows, the slayers are wading in blood mid-thigh.
There were some whose swords were broken or bent with blow on blow:
Empty their hands were of weapons wherewith to smite the foe,
Until of their horns they bethought them, and the trumpets that kindle the fight;
Fiercely they seize them, as maces they swing them with deadly might.
Feet, hands, are the red blades lopping, cleaving body and head:—
"These Franks," cried the fleeing paynims, "be vassals of prowess dread!
The storm of destruction we looked for—lo, on our heads it broke!"
Fast from the battle flee they, turning their backs to our folk,
And the Frank swords lighten behind them, hewing and thrusting amain.
That flight to the camp of Marsila is marked by trails of the slain.

126

Marsila beheld the slaughter of warriors near and far;
And he bade blow up the trumpets, and sound the horns of war.
Himself hath mounted his charger, hath mustered his great array,
And Abismes, their Saracen champion, foremost rides to the fray:—
Than he no viler caitiff in all that company is;
Stained is his soul with treasons, with foulest iniquities:
Not in our God he believeth, nor in Holy Mary's Son;
So dour and grim, he hath jested with no man, hath smiled on none.
Dearer be treason and slaughter to him, the murderous-souled,
Than to have at his feet the treasure of all Galicia's gold.
Blacker than pitch flame-molten was the face of that child of night;
Yet the man was a stalwart vassal, a very madman in fight;
And for this Marsila loved him—as felon to felon is dear,—
And his dragon-standard, to rally his host, did Abismes uprear.
Him the Archbishop beholdeth, and with sudden hate is he filled:
As he gazeth, with vehement longing to smite him his soul is thrilled.
Under his breath full softly he murmured fierce and fell:
"This Saracen, meseemeth, is a miscreant infidel!
But now, if it please God, endeth for him his latest day.
Far liever would I perish than fail to meet him and slay.
I have held in abhorrence the dastard and the deeds of the dastard aye!"

W. C. R.   5

127

Forth the Archbishop rideth to challenge the foe to the fight,
Bestriding the goodly war-horse won from Grossaille by his might
When he slew that king of the Danefolk on the marches of Denmark afar.
Exceeding swift was the charger, and taught all manage of war:
Round-hoofed, his legs clean-moulded, broad-crouped, but short in the thigh,
Deep-ribbed, his tail white-flowing, his proud neck arching high,
Small-eared and tawny-headed, his long mane amber-hued—
Thou scarce shouldst find under heaven another steed so good.
In knightly wise the Archbishop spurred him onward amain:
He shaketh the golden bridle, he casteth loose the rein:
He is charging—he will not slacken his speed till amidst of the field
He meeteth Abismes, and smiteth the boss of the wondrous shield.
With gems is it set; there topaz and amethyst gleam arow,
There diamonds flash out starlike, there burning rubies glow.
In Val-metas was it fashioned by a demon-smith, men say,
And was given to this Abismes of the Emir Galafré.
But now hath Turpin struck it with the lance that spareth not:
Against his blow its splendour availeth not a jot.
Clear through his body the lance-head from breast to back hath passed:
Dead is he hurled from the saddle, and down in a void place cast.
"Montjoy! Montjoy!" he shouted, King Charles's rallying-cry.
Said the Franks: "Ha, that was a gallant deed of chivalry!
The hand of our Archbishop doth the Cross full safely ward.
Would God that of such there were many to stand by the King our lord!"

128

Turned unto Oliver Roland, and cried through the battle-din:
"O thou my friend and companion, art not of my mind herein,
That a true knight is the Archbishop, the flower of chivalry?
Of a truth, there is found none better on earth or under sky.
Right cunning he is in smiting with lance and with long keen blade."
"Yea!" Count Oliver shouted; "haste we then to his aid!"
At his words are the Franks rekindled, rewaketh the fury of war:

Starkly they thrust with the lances, mighty their sword-strokes are.
'Neath the shadow of death are they fighting, grim-hearted and heavy of cheer,
But surely, or ever they perish, will they sell their lives right dear!

128 *a*

Of the Franks of France full many their weapons by this have lost:
Remain but now seven hundred swords in all their host,
Yet aye on the gleaming helmets they smite and hew amain—
Great God in Heaven! how many be the bucklers cleft in twain,
The helms that be shattered, the hauberks whose links asunder are torn!
Feet, wrists, and heads how many by the ruthless steel are shorn!
"By these Franks," cried the paynims, "in pieces hewn are we!
Who turneth not and fleeth, small care for life hath he!"
They uplifted their voices, they shouted: "Haste!—to our help, O King!"
Marsila heard that clamour of hard-pressed ranks outring,
And he cried: "O Father Apollo, I pray thee, succour me!
O Land of France, may Mahomet blast thee utterly!
A curse upon thee! thy people have vanquished mine in fight!
Great Rome this Charles hath conquered, the King of the beard snow-white,
And all Calabria's marches, and Apulia from strand unto strand,
And far Constantinople, and the Saxons' stubborn land.
Far liever would I perish than flee yon Frankish crew!
Strike, paynims! let no Frenchman escape with life from you!
If now he may die, this Roland, Charles loseth his right hand:
If we slay him not, to destruction we and our country are banned."

128 *b*

Now rally the paynims: couching the lance to the onset they leap.
Shivered were bucklers before them, beneath the broadsword's sweep
Cloven were helmets, the hauberk-links asunder sprang:
Steel upon iron was ringing with multitudinous clang:
Sparks from the smitten armour and flame-jets heavenward leapt:
Blood, brains, all round were spattered—who had seen it, had surely wept!
And now was the good Count Roland in sorrow and heaviness
To see those noble vassals fall fast in the battle's stress.

5—2

And he called sweet France to remembrance with a sudden throb of pain:
His thoughts flew far to his uncle, the good King Charlemagne;
And his stubborn pride was abated, from ruth could he not refrain.

128 *c*

But he hardened his heart, and he hurled him into the thick of the fray:
Mightily there is he smiting with neither stint nor stay:
Sword Durendal far-flashing in his hand is dealing death;
Many a shield it cleaveth and pierceth and shattereth;
On mail-rings leaping asunder, on helms it lighteneth down:
Feet, hands, are shorn from the body, heads cleft to the chin from the crown.
How many hundred paynims dead to the earth hath he cast—
Men who were wont to account them mighty in days overpast!

128 *d*

Not afar from his side in the battle doth his comrade Oliver fight:
He chargeth down on the war-press, and starkly doth he smite
With the sword Haltclere, and swiftly in his hands doth it rise and fall:
There is no such brand under heaven, save only Durendal
In the grasp of its lord which is swinging and flashing and hewing still:
Blood streameth from wrist unto shoulder in many a crimson rill.
"There fighteth a noble vassal and loyal!" crieth his friend.
"Alas for the olden friendship! this day must it come to an end.
Ere set of sun in sorrow parted shall be we twain;
Never shall Charles our liege-lord behold us living again;
Never in France such mourning hath been known unto this day:
Many a valiant baron for our souls' repose will pray:
In holy church petitions mid incense-clouds shall rise
That our souls may enter the mansions prepared in Paradise."
Then Oliver slackened bridle, he spurred his good steed on
Through the tangled press of the battle, till to Roland's side he won.
"Thine hand, O friend and companion!" each unto other saith:
"It may hap that I die before thee, but I fail thee not unto death!"

129

What marvel it was to behold them, Roland and Oliver,
As they hewed and lashed with their war-glaives, as Turpin thrust with the spear !
As touching them that perished, the tale of the slain hath been told :
From of old it standeth recorded, in the charters of France enscrolled.
As the ancient chronicle telleth, four thousand they slew, nay more.
Lo, now have the Franks stood victors in mighty battles four ;
But now is the fifth upon them, and grievous it is and sore ;
For all the Franks have fallen by this, save knights three-score.
These only, of twenty thousand, hath God spared until now ;
But, or ever they die, right dearly shall they sell their lives, I trow !

130

Then marked Count Roland how many of the heroes of France lay dead,
And he spake unto his companion, and to Oliver he said :
"My friend and my companion, in God's name, counsel me :
All these good vassals lying dead on the earth dost thou see.
For France the fair and pleasant good cause have we to mourn
That of all these noble barons she is left henceforth forlorn.
Alas, my friend and liege-lord, that thou art afar from us now !"
"My friend and companion," answered Oliver, "well knowest thou,
Hadst thou but hearkened to counsel given of me long ago,
Our King had been here, and had taken vengeance on yonder foe."
"Oliver, friend and brother, may no way yet be found ?
How may we send him tidings of the perils that compass us round ?"
But scornfully Oliver answered : "How know I what should be said ?
Should I stain my name with dishonour ?—rather would I lie dead !"

131

"Behold, I will sound," said Roland, "Olifant mine horn :
His voice unto Charles, who is passing through the mountain-gate, shall be borne,
And so, I give thee assurance, the host of the Franks shall return."
Fiercely Oliver answered : "And foul reproach wilt thou earn,
And the battle-blencher's dishonour upon all thy kin shall be cast,

And deep shame ever-during so long as their life shall last!
What time I bade thee do it, thou wouldst give to my word no heed,
And now, if thou sound, shalt thou sound it in no wise by my rede:
Yea, if thou blow thy war-horn, it shall not be a brave man's deed!
The contrary part hast thou chosen—lo, red are thine hands with blood!"
Answered the Count: "Yea, sword-strokes have I stricken as good knight should."

132

Spake Roland: "Grievous battle against our remnant is set.
Mine horn will I sound; our liege-lord Charles shall hear it yet."
But grimly Oliver answered: "Thereof shalt thou have great shame,
And shalt bring reproach and dishonour on all thy race and name!
When this was my counsel, companion, to hearken thou wouldst not deign:
Had the King been here in season, no hurt had his rearguard ta'en.
But of all the blame no shadow on those far friends doth lie!"
Then cried he in sudden anger: "By this my beard swear I—
If my fair sister Alda again with mine eyes I see,
Never with my consenting shall she in her arms clasp thee!"

133

Made answer Roland: "Wherefore art wroth with me, brother mine?"
Made answer Oliver: "Comrade, the fault is wholly thine!
Valour with prudence tempered unto folly is nowise allied:
Better is courage in measure than reckless rashness of pride.
By thy foolhardy madness the knights of France lie slain!
Never of us his vassals shall Charles have service again.
Our lord, if to me thou hadst hearkened, had been with us long agone,
And so had this lost battle full lightly of us been won,
And yonder King Marsila taken or dead had been.
In an evil day, O Roland, of us was thy prowess seen!
No help shalt thou render hereafter to Charles, to the man most famed
From this to the Day of Judgment: thou wilt die, and France will be shamed;
Nor beyond this day may our loyal companionship longer abide:
Friend from friend in dolour shall be rent ere eventide."
Then each in his ruth for his fellow bitterly wept and sighed.

134

Now the Archbishop heard their contention, and thitherward he spurred
With the spurs of gold his war-horse, and he spake a reproachful word:
"Lords Oliver and Roland, contend not now, I pray
In God's name! See yon Frenchmen: all doomed unto death be they.
What though the horn be sounded?—it cannot avert our doom.
Far off is Charles from our helping, and late should it be ere he come.
Yet—yet, if thou sound the war-horn, even so, perchance, it were good;
For surely will Charles come hither, and be our avenger of blood:
So the caitiffs of Spain from their triumph shall return with little mirth;
And our Franks after that great vengeance shall leap from saddle to earth;
Dead shall they find us lying with limbs all hacked and torn:
On biers shall they lay our bodies by sumpter-beasts to be borne;
And shall raise in sorrow and pity the lamentation-cry;
And in quiet courts of cloisters in peace shall our bodies lie,
Nor wolf nor hound nor wild-boar shall rend us limb from limb."
"Sir, meetly and well hast thou spoken," made answer Roland to him.

134 *a*

Spake Oliver—strength and wisdom o'ermastered anger and scorn—
"Yea," answered he, "Lord Roland, even now do thou sound thine horn;
So Charles shall hear, through the mountain-gate as he marcheth afar,
And so shall he turn backward his marvellous host of war.
So shall the Franks take vengeance for the men of our array
Whom the Saracen hordes in battle have prevailed to smite and to slay;
So shall they take up the bodies of us whose life hath fled,
Nor bear nor lion nor wild-boar shall rend the belovèd dead."
"Sir, courteously and knightly hast thou spoken," Roland said.

135

To his lips now Roland raiseth Olifant, and fast
He graspeth the ivory, putting his whole strength into the blast.
High are the mountain-ridges, the cliffs toss onward afar
Over fifteen leagues the echoes of that wild note of war,

So that of Charles and his vassals all hath been heard the sound.
And the King said, "Hark!—our warriors with battle be compassed round!"
With an evil sneer to his liege-lord Count Ganelon replied:
"Had any save thee, King, spoken, in his throat, I had said, had he lied."

136

But now with pain Count Roland, with striving of strong strain,
With pangs of endeavour, soundeth Horn Olifant again.
From between his lips is streaming the blood bright-crimson now,
And the very bones are rifted of the temples of his brow.
That voice of the great horn crying is beyond all measure great,
And again King Charles hath heard it afar at the mountain-gate.
Duke Naimes withal hath heard it: the Franks are listening.
Said Charles: "'Twas the horn of Roland that I surely heard outring!
He would sound not, except our rearguard into straits of battle were brought."
But Ganelon made answer: "Of battle is there nought!
Behold, by this art thou stricken in years and silver-haired,
And herein may thy words unto nothing but a young child's speech be compared.
Full well, O King, thou knowest Roland's arrogant pride:—
It is marvel that God hath suffered His patience so long to be tried!
Erewhile the burg of Nobles unbidden of thee did he smite:
Forth of its ramparts sallied the Saracen host to the fight,
To the battle against this Roland, thy vassal valiant and true:
All, all with the brand far-famous Durendal he slew.
Then turned he the course of a river, and swept with its waters the plain
Of his freakish humour that slaughter thereon should leave no stain!
Daylong would he go sounding his horn for a single hare:
Even now, I trow, is he making sport for the Twelve Peers there.
Beset is he, quotha?—'neath heaven dare none defy to the fray
This champion of thine—ride onward!—wherefore thus delay?
Press on; for France, for the homeland, lieth far away."

137

The mouth of Roland is bleeding, the bones of his temples are rent:
There was pain and anguished endeavour in the third blast Olifant sent.

But Charles and the Franks have heard it: "Long breath is in that strain
Of the horn!" said the King. Naimes answered: "Verily sore in pain
Is the baron who sounded it: battle they have, right well I know;
And that this traitor knoweth, and fain would deceive thee, I trow!
O King, gird on thine armour, thy rallying war-cry raise:
Haste to the help of thine high-born knights in the perilous place!
Well mayest thou hear that Roland is now in evil case."

138

Thereat the Emperor bade them blow up the horns straightway.
Down leapt the Franks from their horses; they donned their war-array,
Their hauberks and their helmets, and their swords with the hilts of gold;
From their necks hang gleaming bucklers, and long stout spears do they hold,
And gonfalons white and crimson and blue, to the breeze unrolled.
Now mount their chargers the barons all; through the long defiles
They spur them to speed, and ever, through the pass's weary miles,
This man and that to their fellows were crying, and still they said:
"Oh but to look upon Roland, or ever that knight be dead!
Then will we strike full starkly at his side in the battle-throng!"
Alas and alas! what avails it?—they have tarried all too long!

139

The lowering eventide brightens to day: in the sun's sudden rays
Flasheth the mail: lance, helmet and hauberk are all ablaze:
His splendour o'er shields flower-blazoned and gold-fringed gonfalons plays.
Wrathful the Emperor rideth, the Franks with passionate tears
Press on: not a man but is weeping, not a man but for Roland fears.
Now have they seized that traitor by command of the King his lord:
To the scullions of his palace is he given to be kept in ward:
And their chief Charles summoneth, Besgun, and saith to him: "See thou hold
This fellow in ward as a traitor: mine house to my foes hath he sold."
The man hath received him, and haleth where a hundred varlets wait,
Knaves of the spit and caldron, of better or worse estate.
From his lips and his chin for dishonour they pluck away the hair,
And once and again to smite him with the fist doth no man spare.

With rods and with staves are they hailing upon him blow on blow,
And a chain, as when one chaineth a bear, o'er his neck they throw.
On the back of a sorry garron for dishonour the wretch they fling,
And in such wise hold him warded till they render him up to the King.

140

Ah me, how high are the mountains, how huge and gloomy they are!
Deep are the gorges, where torrents are rushing. To vanward afar
And to rearward Charlemagne's trumpets are pealing to answer the horn
Of Roland. The Emperor rideth in wrath; in fury on-borne
Are the Franks, and in anguish: is no man but weepeth and grieveth sore,
And prayeth: " O God, save Roland until we win to the war !
We will mightily smite beside him then !" Vain strivers with fate !
It avails not : they cannot win thither in time—too late, too late !

141

Ever in burning anger Charlemagne rideth on.
His white beard over his hauberk by the wind of his rushing is blown:
The barons of France spur onward in haste; in passionate grief
They mourn that they cannot by Roland be standing, the great war-chief
Who is grappling in mortal combat with the Saracens of Spain;
For if he, their captain, be smitten, who then alive shall remain?
Ah God, for the peerless sixty that now are all his array !
Never was king nor captain who had better knights than they.

141 *a*

On, ever on through the endless pass fast rideth the King.
Overstreaming his armour the silver of his beard is glistering ;
His brow is dark with anger, his eyes are dim with tears.
"Help us, O Holy Mary !" he cries, sore racked with fears :
"Whelmed in floods of affliction am I by Ganelon's hands !
In an ancient chronicle written, I mind me, the record stands
That his ancestors from the beginning were felons foul in grain ;
Their whole life was one treason : Rome's Capitol did they stain
With innocent blood, when Caesar by them was foully slain.

But for this was vengeance taken: to an evil end they came,
When in anguish of bitter torment they died in burning flame.
And the blood of the felons floweth in this foul traitor's frame!
It is he that hath doomed Knight Roland, he that hath ruined mine host!
Ah me, the shield and defender of the land of France is lost!
From mine head my crown hath he taken, of all my glory hath shorn!"
He brake into weeping, his silver beard by his hands is torn;
And the Franks cried: "Woe for us! wherefore were we ever born?"
Onward they spur through the endless pass for the Gates of Spain:
None is there that slacketh his riding, nor any that draweth rein.
But, or ever the host of the helpers have won to the goal, that fight
Shall of Roland be won: Marsila and his men shall be all in flight.

142

Far over mountain and moorland in ruth did Roland glance.
Full many he seeth lying dead of the heroes of France,
And he wept for them and lamented as for good knights valiant and true:
"Ah, noble lords and barons, may God have mercy on you!
Unto your souls may He open the mansions of Paradise,
And lay you to rest on the flowers of the infinite fields of the skies!
Better and loyaller vassals than you may I never see:
Through years on years have ye rendered faithful service to me:
Wide realms and fair your prowess hath bowed 'neath Charlemagne's hand:—
Alas for our lord, that ever he nurtured so goodly a band!
O Land of France, an exceeding pleasant land art thou;
But of all these noble vassals thou sittest widowed now!
O barons of France, of my doing it is that I see you die!—
And now I cannot defend you, for you no help have I!
May the God of Truth be your helper, He who cannot lie!
O Oliver my brother, by thee will I stand alway.
If a foeman do not slay me, the grief of mine heart shall slay!
Now, O my friend, my companion, once more let us on to the fray!"

142 a

Once more up the slopes of the mountain, down the long vales again
He gazeth on those brave vassals, by thousands on thousands slain;

And to these Count Roland pointed, and to Oliver he cried
With a ringing voice: "Fair brother, we must die by our brethren's side!
With these must we lie which be lying here: for our love they have died!
Sweet France, how art thou widowed! The Emperor loseth to-day
His noblest vassals!" For sorrow Roland's face is grey.
Then he turned him, and four times shouted "Montjoy!" the battle-cry:
Horn Olifant he graspeth, and the charge peals loud and high.
Veillantif is he spurring against the paynim horde:
Durendal is he swinging on high, the resistless sword.

143

Charging again is Roland the Count across the field:
Like a wrath-enkindled vassal his sword doth he fiercely wield.
Falbrun de Puy he meeteth, and straightway cleaveth him down,
And four-and-twenty beside him, famous, men of renown.
Ye shall never look on warrior for vengeance more aflame!
As fleeth through the forest from hounds the antlered game,
So before Roland the paynims fled with desperate speed.
That saw the Archbishop, and shouted: "Well struck! O gallant deed!
So valiant should every knight be who bestrideth a goodly steed,
And beareth arms: in battle fierce and fell should he be,
Else do I value his knighthood at less than one straw's fee.
Fitter were he for a shaveling monk in a cloister's shade;
So at the least for our trespass all day long had he prayed."
"Strike!" Roland shouted in answer: "Strike ever! Spare no foes!"
At his words were the Franks reheartened; they struck yet mightier blows.
But the Christians are falling; the remnant ever smaller grows.

144

Who looketh to find no mercy, when ransom is none from death,
That man will defend him in battle unto his latest breath.
And for this cause stand the Frenchmen as lions at bay in fight.
But lo, now cometh Marsila, and he seemeth a gallant knight,
Bestriding his mighty war-horse—Gaignun they name that steed—
And against the good knight Bevon he spurreth his eager speed—

Of Belné and of Dijon that lord was suzerain :—
Crashed through his buckler the lance-head, it rifted the hauberk in twain;
Deep in his body are buried the laps of the gonfalon;
Dead from the saddle straightway is hurled that noble one.
Thereafter Ivoire and Ivon by the hand of Marsila died,
And Girard the lord of Roussillon is laid on the earth at their side.
But thitherward came Count Roland cleaving the battle-tide :
To the paynim he shouted : "Caitiff! God's malison on thee!
Thou hast slain my friends, my companions, hast slain them treacherously!
For this, ere we part, will I smite thee: thou shalt not 'scape mine hand!
Yea, this day shalt thou know it, how named is this my brand!"
So, like a knightly baron, he swoopeth down on the foe,
And the right hand of Marsila hath he swept from the wrist at a blow.
Then one thrust in between them; but dashed was the bright-haired head
At the feet of the King his father, and Jorfaleu fell dead.
Then a cry went up from the paynims : "Help us, O Mahound!
In thee let our avenger on Charlemagne's men be found!
He hath sent against us such felons into this our land of Spain,
That 'neath death's very shadow to flinch from the fight they disdain!"
Then suddenly Saracen shouted "Flee, flee!" unto Saracen :
At the cry unto flight all turned them, a hundred thousand men.
Essay who will to rally or stay them, they turn not again.

144 *a*

Of his right hand King Marsila so is bereft, and his eyes
See Jorfaleu his firstborn, where dead at his feet he lies.
From his arm the useless buckler down to the earth hath he flung,
And to headlong flight his charger with the sharp spurs hath he stung.
Faster and faster Spainward he fleeth with loosened rein,
And with him a hundred thousand are streaming across the plain.
There is none of them all but hath gotten sore wounds in that fierce fray;
And the cry goeth up : "Charles' nephew is victor again this day!"

145

Ah, what avails it ?   Albeit Marsila fleeth afar,
Remaineth his uncle the Caliph still to rekindle the war,
Who is lord of Carthage, Alferna, Garmalie, and the land
Of the Ethiop God-accursèd; and the men of his vassal-band
Be black, with demon-faces broad-browed and monstrous-eyed ;
And of these there be fifty thousand that gather at his side.
Onward the long line rideth proudly and furiously :
Rings from those charging thousands their paynim battle-cry.
"Now shall we receive," cried Roland, "the crown of martyrdom.
O yea, full well I know it, quickly the end shall come.
But cowards are all who sell not dearly their lives to the last !
Strike, good lords, with the burnished blades ! Strike hard, strike fast !
Fight against death approaching, fight for the fleeting life !
Let sweet France not be dishonoured by us in this last strife !
When Charles our liege-lord cometh to this war-crimsoned plain,
And seeth our glorious vengeance, the heaps of paynims slain,
And for each dead vassal seeth slaughtered foes fifteen,
Then will he not refrain him from blessings on us, I ween."

146

When Roland beheld the accursèd, whose faces be blacker of hue
Than ink, and white are only the teeth of the demon-crew,
He spake : "This day shall we surely die, in mine heart I know ;
But a traitor he is who selleth not dearly his life to the foe.
Strike, Franks, for the fight is rekindled !"   And Oliver shouted, " Accurst
Be the laggard !"   Thereat the Frenchmen on those hellish squadrons burst.

147

When the paynims beheld how scanty was the remnant of Franks, with pride
Were their souls uplifted and heartened, and one to another they cried :
"In the wrong is their Emperor proven ! The right is on our side !"
The Caliph spurreth his red-roan steed with the spurs of gold,
And at Oliver's back he coucheth his lance—the treacherous-souled !

Pinned by the cruel spear-shaft to his back is the hauberk bright,
And out through the midst of his breast-bone the lance-point shoots to the light,
Shouted the caitiff in triumph: "Thou hast gotten thy death from me!
In an evil day forsaken by Charles at the pass were ye!
He hath wronged us, but little of glory therefrom or of joy shall he gain;
For in thee alone have I taken vengeance for all our slain!"

148

Full well Oliver knoweth that smitten he is unto death:
On the smiter he turneth—his vengeance nowise lingereth—
On the sword of the steel dark-splendid, Haltclere, hath he tightened his hold—
On the helmet he smiteth the Caliph, on the high-peaked crest of gold.
Shattered the flowers and the gemstones that decked it earthward rain:
From the crown to the teeth that paynim's head hath he cleft in twain.
As the sword from the stroke upswingeth, the stricken falleth dead;
And Oliver shouteth: "Heathen, a curse upon thine head!
I say not that Charles hath nothing lost—but never of thee
Shall boast be made to a leman, nor vaunt in thy seignory
That thou from his hand hast wrested the worth of a farthing-fee,
Or hast done unto me a mischief or to any man beside!"
Thereafter he called unto Roland: "Ho! to mine help!" he cried.

149

Oliver knew that wounded he was unto death, and he turned
To his vengeance, and never sated was the wrath in his soul that burned.
Like a knightly baron smiting through their densest array did he ride,
Shearing through spear-shaft, hauberk, through ankle and wrist and side;
Limb from limb was he hewing—who had seen earth heaped with the slain,
Such an one had remembered how heroes bear them in battle-strain.
The war-cry of Charles he forgat not: "Montjoy!" rang loud and clear;
And to Roland his friend he shouted: "Comrade, to me draw near!
Sundered in sorrow exceeding this day must we be, O brother!"
Then brake they forth into sudden weeping, each for other.

150

On Oliver's face looked Roland; it was death-grey, livid and wan,
And out of his body welling the blood bright-crimson ran
Streaming to earth from the gashes, and ebbed his life therethrough:
"Ah God!" cried Roland despairing, "I know not what to do!
Brother, alas for the glory that all thy prowess hath won!
Thy like shall be seen not hereafter, O knighthood's paragon!
O ruined France, of thine heroes forlorn, O land undone!
And alas for the loss that befalleth our King by this last blow!"
And with that word swooned Knight Roland, drooped over his saddle-bow.

151

Aswoon in his saddle sits Roland; and Oliver, wounded to death,
His eyes all dimmed by the blood-drain, nought clearly distinguisheth
Nor near nor far, and he seeth men but as shapes in a mist;
And he reeleth against his comrade thus, and, or ever he wist,
His blind stroke smiteth the gemstones and the gold on his helm, and asunder
Cleaveth it down to the nose-piece, yet touched not the head thereunder.
Then looked on him Roland the smitten, and sweetly and soft spake he:
"Dost know whom thou smitest, my comrade?—Roland, who loveth thee!
Never, in joy or in sorrow, have I forgotten thee:
Never hast thou defied me by a word of enmity!"
"I hear thee speak," said his comrade, "but thy face I cannot see.
God look upon thee! I have smitten thee—O forgive it to me!"
"No hurt have I gotten," said Roland: "I forgive thee before God's face."
On each other's necks then fell they in love's long last embrace.

152

Oliver feels death's anguish; now turn in his head his eyes;
Fail hearing and sight: he dismounteth, on earth looking eastward he lies.
He lifteth his voice in confession of sin; he hath raised unto heaven
Clasped hands, crying: "Lord, unto me be a place in thy Paradise given!
Bless Charles, bless France the belovèd; and above all men bless thou
Roland my comrade!"—his heart-beats fail; from his head slips now

His helmet; to earth has he sunken with limp limbs—all is o'er!
Dead is the Count. Knight Roland gazeth and weepeth sore.
Ye shall find in the wide world never a man that sorroweth more.

153

When Roland beheld how his comrade with his face to the east lay dead,
Sighingly, tenderly over the fallen he mourned, and he said:
"Alas for my friend and my brother! woe's me for the dauntless-souled!
Ah for the years of our friendship, happy days untold!
Unto me hast thou never imagined despite, neither I unto thee!
And now thou art dead, it is treason in me that I live—woe's me!"
Then for sorrow the Lord of the Marches heart-broken swooneth away
On Veillantif his war-horse; but the stirrups of gold upstay
His feet, that he falls not earthward, though he heavily reel and sway.

154

But scarce revived is Roland from his swoon, than the knight is ware
Of exceeding grievous disaster; for slain the Franks lie there:
Yea, dead are they all, save only the Archbishop and Walter of Hum,
Who by this from the mountain-ridges to that main battle had come.
On the heights had he long contended against the thousands of Spain,
Till, overborne by the paynims, all his men lay slain.
In his heart's despite, he descendeth of sore need into the plain;
And he calleth for help on Roland: "O Count most noble, say
Where art thou, hero?—never by thy side have I known dismay.
Behold, it is Walter that calleth, who laid Prince Maelgut low,
The nephew of Droün the ancient of the head and beard of snow.
To thy friendship by valiant service of a vassal did I attain;
But pierced is now my buckler, my spear is knapped in twain;
Mine hauberk is hewn in pieces and torn in battle-strain;
My body with thrust of lances hath been wounded once and again.
Die shall I surely; but dearly will I sell my life ere then!"
Straightway known unto Roland was he who spake that word:
He turned his rein; through the battle swiftly to meet him he spurred.

W. C. R. 6

154 a

"Lord Walter," cried Count Roland, "thou hast fought hard battle, I trow.
Thou hadst many a warrior-vassal, a thousand knights hadst thou
Of me: now therefore restore them, for my need of them is sore."
Made answer Walter: "Never shalt thou look upon these any more.
On the dolorous field I left them: Saracens there we found;
Turks and Armenians and Arabs and Persians encompassed us round,
Bedouins, Algolancians—such battle of giants we fought,
No paynim of all shall vaunt him ever of deeds there wrought,
For their threescore thousand be lying dead on the field of blood,
And there be our Franks all lying whelmed 'neath the nations' flood.
But the steel of our brands hath avenged us!—see, rent be the links of my mail:
Wounds have I many; on shoulders, on flanks did the fierce blows hail.
The blood bright-crimson is welling from me on every side;
My strength from all my body fleets like an ebbing tide;
I am marked for death of a surety, well mine heart doth know.
My lord, I am thy vassal, allegiance to thee I owe:
I pray thee, forbear to blame me from that lost field who ride!"
"Not I will blame thee ever!" unto him Count Roland replied.
"With travail and pain, O comrade, thou hast striven a gallant strife:
But now be thou mine helper to thy last breath of life."

155

In sorrow and anger Roland down on the press of the foe
Chargeth and smiteth: swiftly a score hath he laid low,
And the Archbishop five, and Walter seven, of the warriors of Spain.
Then a cry went up from the paynims: "These villains be knighthood's stain!
Take good heed, O ye barons, that alive they go not hence!
Let none be held to ransom who have wrought to us such offence!
A traitor be he accounted who flincheth from the fight,
And a recreant he who shall suffer but one to escape our might!"
Then roared the clamour of onset like the roar of an angry sea,
And from every hand those myriads leapt on the aweless three.

156

Full fearless is Count Roland, haughty and grim of mood ;
And Walter of Hum aye bears him as a knight exceeding good ;
A hero is the Archbishop, a paladin battle-tried :
No one of the three gives backward a foot from a comrade's side.
But ever with might overwhelming the paynim ranks press round :
Of the Saracens a thousand from the saddle have leapt to the ground,
And yet on their horses mounted be twoscore thousand foes ;
Yet none of all those myriads with the terrible Three dared close,
But they hurled the spear keen-pointed, they sped from afar the lance,
The javelin, the dart, the arrow, the pike, at the heroes of France.
Beneath those shafts down-hailing falls Walter dead on the field :
Turpin of Reims is smitten, pierced through and through is his shield ;
His dinted helmet is shattered, himself hath wounds in the head ;
Rent is his hauberk, the link-mail hangs in many a shred ;
Four lances have pierced his body from the hands of dastards sped ;
And now his gallant war-horse beneath his lord sinks dead.
Ah God, what sorrow, when fallen upon him his rider lies !
Now be his shield and defender the glorious Lord of the Skies !

157

Turpin of Reims hath fallen, pierced through by lances four ;
But he leapt to his feet right swiftly, that baron wounded sore :
He beheld where yet fought Roland, he ran to the hero's side :
"Not yet, not yet am I vanquished !" the stout Archbishop cried :
"Never was loyal vassal that yielded ere he died !"
The sword of the steel dark-splendid, Almice, from the scabbard flashed :
In the midst of that sea of foemen he plunged, he thrust and lashed—
A thousand strokes !—thereafter said Charles : "Not a foe did he spare !"
For there lay four hundred paynims in a death-ring round him there,
Wounded, pierced through the body, their heads from their shoulders shorn,
As the ancient chronicle telleth ; and another his witness hath borne,
Saint Giles, who was there in the battle, through whom were miracles wrought
Of God. To the cloister of Laon the record thereof he brought.
Whosoever gainsayeth his witness, of the truth he knoweth nought.

6—2

158

Knightly he smites, Count Roland, in sweat and in fervent heat;
But with throbbings and anguished thrillings ever his temples beat,
Where that great blast on the war-horn had cleft the bones in twain;
And aye for his lord Charles' coming he yearneth exceeding fain.
Then Olifant once more grasped he: he blew—O feebly he blew!
But afar the Emperor halted, and hearkened thereunto:
"God!—woe for us, barons, for Roland has sorest need of us now!
So faint was the sound of his war-horn, that his life fast faileth, I trow.
Would ye fain be in time for his helping, spur onward your chargers fast:
Sound trumpets; all through the war-host peal out a mighty blast!"
Pealed clarions threescore thousand; the shattering blare shrills high,
That the mountains echo in thunder, the shuddering valleys reply.
And the paynims heard: from their false lips did the laughter of triumph die—
"It is Charlemagne!—lo, he is coming!" each unto other they cry.

159

"The Emperor"—shrieked the pagans—"the Emperor draweth near!
That is the blast full surely of the clarions of France that we hear!
Woe to us, if Charles cometh! If Roland die not, again
Shall the war awake!—lost ever then is our land of Spain!"
Four hundred have banded them, helmet on head, the mightiest they
In the paynim host, and on Roland in onslaught of furious fray
Hurl they: in sooth is the hero sorely bestead this day.

160

On their onset he looked, and his prowess and pride swelled up to the height:
He turned upon them, as a lion when fury enkindleth his might.
He shall not be recreant while beateth his heart—death rather than flight!
His thighs gripped Veillantif's saddle, with the rowels of gold he spurred:
In fierce wrath into the war-press he charged of the paynim herd:
Charged Archbishop Turpin beside him: the Saracens "Fly, friends, fly!"
Shrieked each unto other—"the trumpets of France, we have heard them cry!
Lo, he returneth, the mighty King—lo, Charlemagne nigh!"

161

Hateful to Roland ever was the coward, and he whose pride
In the heart of a churl was rooted, and the knight who dared not abide
All odds, like a loyal vassal.   Now unto Turpin he cried:
"Sir, thou art afoot, and mounted am I: for love of thee, still
Here will I stay; together will we share the good and the ill!
For no man alive will I leave thee: they shall learn, this paynim horde;
The names of Almice the War-glaive, and of Durendal the Sword!"
And the Archbishop cried: "A felon is he who should now fail thee!
After to-day's fight never another again shall we see;
But Charles draweth nigh to avenge us, to punish treachery."

162

But the paynims faltered, crying: "To calamity, lo, we were born!
This day is a day of ruin; accurst was the light of its morn!
Our chiefest barons have perished, our men of renown have we lost,
And Charles the victorious war-lord draweth nigh with his mighty host.
We can hear the Frankish clarions outpealing loud and clear,
And the voice of a multitude shouting "Montjoy! Montjoy!" we hear.
So dauntless is this Count Roland, that never human foe
May vanquish him—hurl we our lances, if perchance we may lay him low.
Leapt javelins, darts, spears, lances; fast flew the arrow-wings,
Till pierced was the shield of Roland, and shattered its plates, and the rings
Of his hauberk were broken asunder, and its golden garnishings;
Yet point nor edge of weapon the flesh of his body hath found.
But Veillantif his war-horse is stricken with wound on wound,
Even thirty, till under his master he sinketh dead to the ground.
But the last of the foe are fleeing, and they leave him standing alone,
Alone on his feet, Count Roland, mid thousands overthrown.

162 *a*

Fast are they fleeing, the paynims; in utterest panic they cry
Each unto other: "Roland hath conquered! Now draweth nigh
The Emperor of a surety! Hark—there the war-horns pealed

Of the Franks! He is doomed to destruction who waiteth them here on the field!
So many kings most noble hath he bowed beneath his sway,
That Mahound no more may defend us, nor help in the evil day.
We have lost, we have lost the goodly land of Spain for aye,
Except the Emir from the far land come to our aid straightway."

163

The paynims are fleeing: in anguish of rage fast Spainward they fly:
But not now Roland pursueth, for dead doth his war-horse lie.
Afoot must he bide, be he willing or no: he seeketh now
Archbishop Turpin: his helmet of gold he unlaced from his brow;
Of his bright steel hauberk he stripped him, his tunic to shreds did he rend,
And he stanched and bound with the fragments the gaping wounds of his friend.
Close to his breast he clasped him, and on green grass gently laid
In such fashion that over his fevered visage the cool breeze played;
And he spake, and his voice was gentle and low, as Roland prayed:
"Ah, suffer me, noble baron: the friends that we held so dear,
Dead are they all, our companions; yet we may not abandon them here.
Hence will I, and seek and discern them, wheresoever they be,
And hitherward bring them, and lay them before thee orderly."
"Go thou," replied the Archbishop, "and return unto me again.
Thank God, unto thee this stricken field and to me doth remain."

164

So Roland hath turned him; he fareth alone through the field of fight:
He searcheth by yawning gorges, he seeketh by precipice-height.
To Ivoire he came and to Ivon, with Gerier Gerin he found;
Berenger, Otho, Anseïs and Sansun lay stretched on the ground:
Upon Engelier he lighted, the Gascon war-renowned,
And Girard of Roussillon, a grey head glory-crowned.
Unto the dying Archbishop one after other he bare,
And before his knees he ranged them, the slain chiefs, orderly there.
The Archbishop no more could refrain him, but forth into weeping he brake,
And his hand he solemnly lifted, and the word of his blessing he spake.
Then, after the benediction, he mourned with compassionate sighs:

THE SONG OF ROLAND

"Ah lords, ill lot is your portion! May the glorious God to the skies
Receive your spirits, and set them mid the flowers of His Paradise!
Ah me, and mine own death cometh!—it cometh with anguish of pain:
On my King shall I look not hereafter, on the splendour of Charlemagne!"

165

Roland departeth, he searcheth the field: 'neath a pine-tree's shade
Nigh to a briar, he findeth his comrade Oliver laid.
To his heart doth he strain him; with failing strength then pacing the field,
The Archbishop he seeks, and beside them, the rest of the Peers, on a shield,
Layeth his friend. The Archbishop hath blessed and absolved them all.
High surgeth the tide of his sorrow, his tears of compassion fall:
"Fair Oliver, O my comrade," cried Roland, "thou wast son
Of the Count of Rivier's marches, Reignier the mighty one:
If need were a lance to shiver, or a buckler in pieces to hew,
Or to burst through the hauberk whose shattered links asunder flew,
Or to give to the good leal counsel, proud traitors in dust to bow,
Never in any country was better knight than thou."

166

Now when Count Roland beheld them, these Twelve Peers lying dead,
And his best-belovèd comrade Oliver, straightway he shed
Tears of sorrow draining his heart, till his face waxed white:
So sore was his anguish, that longer he could not stand upright;
He reeled, and swooning earthward he fell in his own despite.
"Alas for thee!" sighed the Archbishop, "alas for thee, noble knight!"

167

When Turpin beheld how Roland on earth in a dead swoon lay,
Such sorrow was his, as never had he known before that day.
He outstretcheth his hand, he taketh the great horn Olifant:
Now at Roncesval ran a brooklet adown the hill's long slant;
Thither would he, unto Roland to give of the quickening flood.
He strained with sorest endeavour, till at last on his feet he stood;
And thither he turned him, reeling with tottering steps and slow.

But so utter-weak is he waxen, that he may no further go,
So wholly strengthless, by reason of all that life-blood lost,
That, ere a furlong's measure of that field of death is crossed,
His heart-beats fail, and he falleth heavily down on his face;
And now with anguish cometh his own death on him apace.

168

From his swoon Count Roland reviveth, on his feet he standeth upright;
But passing great is his sorrow as he looketh o'er plain and height;
For beyond his other companions on the green grass lying he sees
The noble Archbishop, steward of God's deep mysteries.
He confesseth his sins, looking upward with clasped hands raised to the skies:
He prayeth that God may vouchsafe him entrance to Paradise.
He is dead—he hath died in the service of Charlemagne his lord.
By the edge of his sword in battle, by the power of the heart-stirring Word,
'Gainst the foes of the Truth its champion through life had he stood fast.
His holy benediction God grant unto him at the last!

168 *a*

When Roland beheld the Archbishop lying dead and alone,
Never such grief, save only for Oliver, had he known;
And he uttered a wail heart-rending, as with bloodless lips he cried:
"Ride, Charles of France, ride hither; at thy uttermost speed O ride!
At Roncesval at thy coming with thine own eyes shalt thou see
Havoc of us thy vassals, and thine own calamity.
Ha, but the King Marsila far more of his own hath lost!
For one of our slain there be lying a hundred dead of his host.

169

Roland the Count beholdeth the Archbishop dead on the plain.
Through the wound in his side wide-gaping his bowels looked forth, and the brain
Oozed over his face 'neath his forehead. On his breast 'twixt his shoulders twain
His crossed hands, white and shapely, with reverence Roland lays;
Then, after the wont of his country, lamenting he speaketh his praise:
"Ah gentle knight, ah scion of lineage proud and high,

To the hands of Him I commit thee who is glory-throned in the sky.
Never man shall be found who in service to Him so fervent hath been:
Nay, since men saw the Apostles, such prophet hath no man seen
The cause of the Cross to champion, to turn men away from their sin.
May thy soul from the pains of the cleansing fires exemption win,
And wide be the Paradise-portals opened to welcome it in !"

170

By this Count Roland feeleth that death is exceeding near:
From the skull his brains are oozing, they droop by either ear.
He prayed unto God for his comrades—"O take them home to thy rest !"
To Gabriel the Angel thereafter a prayer for himself he addressed.
Then, that none for its loss may reproach him, he taketh the wondrous Horn,
And Durendal the war-glaive in his other hand is borne.
Then, farther than a quarrel from a crossbow shot may fly,
Towards Spain, the land of the foemen, he staggereth painfully:
To the height of a hill he ascended; under a green tree there
Four steps of snowy marble of a vanished shrine there were.
Thereby upon the greensward he fell down heavily,
Swooning away:—the shadows of death are very nigh !

171

High is the hill, and exceeding tall be the trees thereon,
And those four steps of marble in the sinking sun's light shone.
There on the green grass Roland the Count in a dead swoon lay.
Now a certain Saracen marked him, spying from far away,
A wretch who had counterfeited death, had cowered mid the slain,
And all his face and his body had smeared with gory stain.
Lo, now to his feet hath he risen, he hasteneth thitherward.
Goodly he was and stalwart and brave, that paynim lord;
And his pride swelled up, and his deadly wrath, as he laid his grip
On the body and armour of Roland, and cried with vaunting lip:
"Vanquished is Charlemagne's nephew !—to Arabia hence will I bear
This sword !" His hand hath clutched it—but it chanced that he plucked at a hair
Of the hero's beard, and Roland thereof was dimly ware.

172

Then suddenly felt Roland that one was taking his sword:
He lifted his heavy eyelids, he spake to the thief one word:
"Not thou art one of the vassals my fellows, well I wot!"
Horn Olifant still was he grasping, firm-purposed to lose it not;
Therewith on the helm of the caitiff so mighty a blow did he deal,
That his head and its bones were shattered within the shattered steel;
And the eyeballs of the stricken started forth of his head,
And down at the feet of the hero fell that paynim dead,
And he said: "Thou dastard pagan, how then wast thou so bold
As on Roland's body, rightly or wrongly, so to lay hold?
For a fool shall he count thee, whoso shall hear this story told!
Lo, now is mine Olifant's bell-mouth shattered by that stark blow,
And the gold thereof and the gemstones lie strewn on the earth below."

173

Roland is ware of the coming of death: with such might as he may
He upriseth, his strength hath he rallied—O me, but his face is grey!
Sword Durendal bared he graspeth: before him a brown rock rose;
In sorrow and wrath he smiteth thereon ten giant blows.
Clasheth the steel unshivered; no, not a dint may ye see.
"Help, Holy Mary!" he crieth: "brave Durendal, woe is thee!
From thee must I part, and thine honour is dear to me as mine own;
With thee have I fought such battles, such realms for my King have I won,
For Charles of the beard of silver! May none that from foemen would flee
Possess thee! While life is within me, thou shalt not be wrested from me.
Long time in the grasp of a vassal hast thou flashed, of a knight without stain,
Such an one as in France, in the Free Land, shall never be found again."

174

Now once more smiteth Roland on the lintel's gleaming flint:
Clasheth the steel unshivered; nay, it hath ta'en no dint.
Then ware was the Count that he could not break it against that stone,
And low to his heart he murmured, and he brake into bitter moan:
"O Durendal, steel all-flawless, how to the sun dost thou flame!
Charles stood in the Morian Valley, when an angel from Heaven came,

And bade him from God to give thee unto a captain tried:
Then thee did the King, the noble and mighty, gird to my side.
Anjou by thee did I win him, Bretagne, won Poitou and Maine,
Won Normandy, land of freemen, Provence did I win, Aquitaine;
Lombardy, all the Romagna, Bavaria, Flanders I won,
Hungary, Poland; and homage Constantinople hath done;
Bohemia, Apulia, Calabria, and all the land of Spain,
The realm of Malva, Palermo, Obria, Ormuraine.
Saxony doeth his pleasure, and Iceland for him did I gain;
Scotland withal and England were made of his royal domain.
O goodly marches I conquered for the King of the beard of snow!
And now for my sword is my spirit in heaviness and woe.
Oh to be dead, or ever this fell to a paynim foe!
Forefend, O God our Father, that France such shame should know!"

175

The dark-brown flint he smiteth more starkly than tongue may record:
Clasheth the steel unbroken, and leaps back heavenward.
Then ware was the Count that he could not break it on any stone,
And low to his heart he murmured, and he brake into bitter moan:
"In thine hilt of gold thou hast wondrous relics, O sacred and fair;
A tooth of Saint Peter, Saint Basil's blood, Lord Denis's hair:
Yea, of the Virgin Mary's vesture a thread is there.
Nay, nay, this shame shall be never that a paynim shall own such brand!
Thou canst not, thou must not be wielded save by a Christian hand.
O battles by thee achievèd, O lands by thee bowed down
'Neath Charles of the beard snow-sprinkled, for my Emperor's wealth and renown!
Never may any man grasp thee who hath quailed at the face of a foe!
O God, forefend that sweet France should in shame be bowed so low!"

176

When Roland was ware that the fingers of death on his frame were laid,
That down from his head they were stealing to his heart, that its beating was stayed,
On the green grass under a pine-tree his body in haste did he lay
Breast-downward; the Sword beneath him and the Horn hath he hidden away.

Dying, his face he turneth to that wide land of Spain;
And this did he by reason that his soul was exceeding fain
That Charles and all his people should testify, seeing him so,
That he died, that noble baron, like a conqueror, face to the foe.
He confesseth all his transgressions, both small and great, and his glove
He uplifteth in penitent homage to God, for a token thereof.

177

Now Roland perceiveth surely that the tide of his life ebbeth low,
On the hill-crest lying and facing Spain the land of the foe;
His breast with his hand he smiteth—"Forgive my sins, O God,
For the sake of thy Might and thy Mercy! O take away the load
Of my small and my great transgressions, from the hour when I first drew breath,
Till the day when overtaken I am by the feet of death!"
Unto God he uplifted the gauntlet of his right hand as he cried;
And an angel from Heaven descended, and stood unseen by his side.

178

Under a pine lay Roland the Count, looking Spainward he lay;
And he called to remembrance many and many a thing that day—
Lands won, sweet France he remembered, the faces of kinsfolk withal,
And Charlemagne his liege-lord, who had fostered him aye in his hall,
And the leal true Franks: and he could not choose but weep and sigh.
Yet the need of his soul he forgat not, and for pardon to God did he cry:
"Father of Truth, who dost lie not, who didst summon to life from the dead
Lazarus, who mid the lions didst cover Daniel's head,
Whose Form by those Three Children in the fiery furnace stayed,
Who didst make all-sinless Mary, the holy Mother-maid,
Who didst for our transgressions thy life on the cross outpour,
And on the third day risen art alive for evermore,
O Father, my soul deliver: from the perils redeem it thou,
Perils that come of transgressions that have stained my life ere now!"
His right hand's iron gauntlet unto God he upraised as he spake,
And out of his hand that token of homage doth Gabriel take.
Then slowly, softly sinketh his head on his arm upcast;

His hands in prayer are folded—now to his end hath he passed.
God sendeth to him of His Angels; His holy Cherubs are these,
Saint Raphael, Saint Michael who saveth men tossed on perilous seas,
And with these Saint Gabriel floateth afar through sundering skies,
And they bear Count Roland's spirit to the rest of Paradise.

179

Dead is Roland, his spirit to heaven hath God brought home.
But now unto Roncesval's stricken field is the Emperor come:
Not a highway he findeth, nor footpath, void place, nor ell of ground,
No, not a footbreadth, but paynim and Frank dead there be found.
Then Charlemagne cried in his anguish: "Fair nephew, where art thou?
Where is the stout Archbishop, and where Count Oliver now?
Where Gerier and Gerin his comrade, and Otho and Berengier?
Ivoire and Ivon, where be they, the men whom I held so dear?
Unto Engelier what hath befallen, the lord of Gascony,
And to Sansun the Duke? And Anseïs the proud knight, where is he?
Where Girard of Roussillon, the white-haired captain of war?
Even all those Twelve Companions whom I left behind me afar?"
What avails it? No voice replieth, none living answereth.
"Ah God! sore indignation have I," the Emperor saith,
"That I might not be here when the trumpets of battle first gave breath!"
His beard with his fingers he teareth, like a man whose wrath is grim:
Tears gush from his eyes; the Frankish knights are weeping with him,
Yea, warriors twenty thousand on earth lie swooning for grief:
Stirred with exceeding compassion is Naimes the old war-chief.

180

No knight was there, neither baron, who wept not sore in ruth;
They wept for their brothers, their nephews, for sons cut off in their youth:
For friends and for liege-lords wept they, and many swooning fell
On the earth. Then Naimes the war-lord did worshipfully and well;
For first to the Emperor spake he: "My Lord, look far before,
There mayest thou see the dust-cloud up from the highways soar
Two leagues afront: there be thousands there of the paynim breed.

Wilt not ride after, for wreaking of vengeance for this foul deed?"
"Ah God!" cried Charles, "already too far away be they!
Now help ye me for maintaining of mine honour and right this day!
Of all sweet France the flower from me have they reft away!"
Then the King commanded Otun and Gebuin, captains of France,
And withal the good count Milo, and Tedbald lord of Reims:
"Guard well this field of slaughter, with the vales and the heights all round.
Leave ye our dead ones lying thus as they are on the ground;
Take heed no lion approach them, nor any beast soe'er;
Nay, not so much as a foot-page or a squire shall venture there:
I forbid you to suffer that any of all men touch our slain
Till the hour when God shall vouchsafe us to return to the field again."
And they lovingly answered and humbly: "This will we do, just Lord."
And they took to them knights a thousand, and so kept watch and ward.

181

Then, at the Emperor's bidding, their challenge the war-horns cried,
And with his great host forward did that kingly baron ride.
Full soon on the tracks of the fleers of Spain came they, and in haste,
Thousands as one man riding, the traitor horde they chased.
Then marked the King how swiftly the shadows of eventide fell:
On the green grass in a meadow straightway he sprang from selle,
And he kneeled on the earth all lowly, and to God the Lord he prayed
That the course of the sun in heaven might for a space be stayed,
That the feet of the night might linger, and the day abide there still.
And behold, that Angel which ofttimes revealed unto him God's will
Cried: "Charles of France, ride onward! The light shall fail thee not.
Lost unto thee are the flower of sweet France, well I wot;
But now mayest thou avenge thee on the guilty people of Spain."
Our King, when he heard that promise, sprang on his horse again.

182

Lo, God for Charlemagne's helping a mighty miracle wrought:
The sun in his place in the heaven unmoving abode; fell not
Over the earth night's mantle, and tarried still the day.

Fast, fast the paynims are fleeing, but the Franks pursue them aye;
And now in the Vale of Shadows they overtake their flight.
On, on unto Saragossa they thrust them, they smite and smite,
Slaying and slaying ever with terrible vengeance-blows.
They bar each highway and byway; all paths of escape they close,
And the water of the Ebro before their feet doth run:
It is marvellous-deep, swift-rushing; barge, dromond or boat is there none!
To Tervagant and to Mahomet and Apollo cried they to aid;
Then leapt they into the water—but all in vain had they prayed.
The most of the knights, heavy-weighted by their armour, suddenly
Sank: some there were that struggled back to the bank—to die.
Others there were that drifted far down, or ever they sank:
Ha! but the strongest swimmer at last the death-draught drank.
Drowned were they all, in anguish perishing wretchedly,
While shouted the Franks: "To your sorrow Knight Roland did ye see!"

183

So now, when ware was our liege-lord that dead were all the foe,
Full many slain, but the more part whelmed in the stream's swift flow,
And beheld how his knights had gotten exceeding goodly prey,
From the selle on his feet down lighted our noble King straightway,
And he bent the knee, and he rendered thanks unto God on high;
And behold, when again he had risen, the sun had dropped from the sky.
Then the Emperor spake: "'Tis the camping-hour of evenfall;
O'er late is it now to be marching back unto Roncesval.
Our steeds be weary and wayworn; ease them of rein and selle,
And turn them loose, to refresh them and graze by mead and dell."
And the knights of France made answer: "Sire, thou counsellest well."

184

The Emperor hath camped him on the upland wide and waste
Twixt Ebro and Valterna: the Franks leap down in haste,
They take from the steeds the saddles and the reins bestarred with gold,
And they leave them to graze at their pleasure on the green grass of the wold,
For in sooth none other provision might any there behold.

Then, utterly forwearied, on the earth they cast them, and slept:
Fear was there none of foemen, and little watch they kept.

185

The Emperor hath couched him in a meadow; his mighty spear
By his good grey head is planted: this night his warrior-gear
Will he not put off from his body; in his bright-fringed hauberk yet
Is he clad, on his brows is his helmet laced all gold-beset.
He is girded with Joyeuse—never was the like of that marvellous blade,
For the rainbow's changeful splendours daily adown it played.
Oft have we heard the story of the lance wherewith our Lord,
As He hung on the cross, was piercèd: in the pommel of that sword
Its point, by God's grace given unto Charles to have and to hold,
Was set, and the steel most holy sealed in the heart of the gold;
And by reason of this high honour, and by reason of this great grace,
The name Joyeuse was given to the Sword of the whole world's praise.
Never let any baron of France forget that name,
For from that sword, thus hallowed, "Montjoy!" our war-cry came;
And for this cause never was nation could stand against the same.

186

Clear is the night, bright shineth the moon; Charles unto his rest
Hath turned him; but sorrow for Roland and Oliver still on his breast
Lieth, a heavy burden, and grief for the Twelve Peers dead,
And for all those Frankish heroes whose lives were in blood outshed
At Roncesval; and he weepeth, he findeth no heart's ease,
And he prayeth God the Redeemer to save the souls of these.
Now spent is the King and weary with trouble passing sore:
Into deep sleep hath he fallen, for he can endure no more.
O'er all the meadows are sleeping the Franks in the hush of night.
In all that host no war-horse hath strength to stand upright:
If any would graze, it croppeth the grass as it lieth at rest.
Who is taught in the school of hardship hath learnt life's lesson best.

187

Heavily Charles is sleeping as a man with toil forspent;
And lo, Saint Gabriel the Angel down to him God hath sent,
And hath bidden him keep watch over the Emperor while he slept.
So all night long his station by his head that Angel kept,
And foreshowed unto him in a vision a battle yet to be fought:
Much presage of travail and anguish is therewithal inwrought.
For Charles in his dream was gazing at a sky all lowering cloud
Whence thunders were crashing, with hailstones, and winds were shrieking loud,
Storms bursting, marvellous tempests, with fires of lightning-flame;
And suddenly on his war-host all these descending came.
Burning are all the spear-staves of cornel-wood and of ash;
Molten are golden bosses of shields by the levin-flash:
Twisted are brand and spear-head, red in the fervent heat,
Crackle the hauberks and helmets as the flames upon them beat.
In grievous straits he beholdeth his knights in that wild hour,
For bears and leopards against them come, and are fain to devour,
There are serpents and vipers upcoiling, dragons and demons are there,
And griffins thrice ten thousand fly through the noisome air.
There is none of them all but rusheth on his host, till, sore afraid,
The Franks in his dream are crying: "O Charlemagne, come to our aid!"
And the King in his great compassion and sorrow is fain to go
To their help, but a mighty hindrance barreth his path, for lo,
Out of a forest a mighty lion rusheth on him,
A lion fierce and furious, and haughty of spirit and grim.
Upon Charles's very body he leapeth, athirst for his life;
And like wrestlers twain they grapple, and strain in deadly strife.
But he knoweth not which shall be victor: all fades into darkness deep:
And still the Emperor slumbers, he wakeneth not from sleep.

188

Before the eyes of the sleeper did another vision pass:
In his dream on the steps of his palace at Aix in France he was.
By two chains bound was he holding a bear; but out of Ardennes,

The forest, he saw forth rushing against him bears thrice ten,
And, each with a man's voice speaking, to the King loud cried they all:
"Sire, yield him to us! Not seemly it is that he be thy thrall!
Our kinsman he is, and bounden we are for his help to stand!"
Then forth of his palace a greyhound rushed on the grisly band;
And of all those bears the hugest his fangs by the throat have caught,
And there amidst its fellows on the grass they grappled and fought.
Charles watcheth that strange conflict till the vision fadeth away;
And the victor the Angel revealed not: so he slept till the breaking of day.

189

Fled is the King Marsila to Saragossa-town:
Under the shade of an olive from his horse he lighteth down.
His sword, his helm, and his mail-coat to his servants giveth he,
And he casteth him down on the greensward in utter misery.
He hath lost his right hand wholly, for the arm from the shoulder is shorn;
And for loss of blood he swooneth, by anguish overborne.
Above him his queen is bending, and there doth Bramimunde pour
Lamentation forth with weeping, for her grief is passing sore.
And mourners there in his garden thrice ten thousand meet,
His vassals, and wail out curses on Charles and on France the sweet.
Then rush they thence to Apollo, where his image stands in a cave,
And hotly they reproach him, and with mad revilings rave:
"False god! now why hast thou shamed us with such dishonouring?
Wherefore hast brought confusion of face on our lord the King?
Who serveth thee well, with evil guerdon dost thou requite!"
They tear from him crown and sceptre, and up to a column's height
By the hands they hang him, thereafter they trample him 'neath their feet,
And with great staves now that image to a trunk misfeatured they beat.
From Tervagant take they his ruby, and into a ditch they throw
Mahomet, where foul swine rend him, and dogs hale to and fro.

190

By this from his swoon Marsila the King revived, and he bade
Bear him away to his vaulted chamber, wherein portrayed
On the walls, and cunningly carven, was bright-hued imagery.

Queen Bramimunde there stood weeping; with exceeding bitter cry
She teareth her hair, and bewaileth herself thus misery-bowed:
Then in frenzied lamentation again she crieth aloud:
" Ah Saragossa, orphaned of him whose kingly sway
Hath warded and ruled thee! Traitors our gods have shown them to-day,
Forasmuch as they have failed him, have forsaken my lord in the fray!
Remaineth the Emir only: a recreant is he, I trow,
If he come not hither to battle against this stubborn foe,
Who be so death-defiant that nought for their lives do they care;
And their Emperor snowy-bearded, mad-reckless to do and to dare,
If battle there be, will never flee from the face of a foe.
Ah, sorrow it is and pity that none may lay him low!"

191

Now Charles by his mighty puissance for seven full years in Spain
Hath warred: he hath stormed her castles, and many a city hath ta'en,
And thereof upon King Marsila sore perplexity came.
In the first of the years had he written letters, and sealed the same,
And to Baligant he sent them, to the city of Babylon—
He was that ancient Emir who lived long ages agone,
Lived long ere Virgil and Homer, and, when they were dead, lived on—
By these he prayed that war-lord that he for his helping would take
His journey to Saragossa; else, he must needs forsake
His gods and all the idols that he wont to adore, must bow
At the Christian font baptismal, and to Charles allegiance vow.
In a far land Baligant dwelleth, and long hath he delayed;
Yet now hath he summoned the war-host of the forty realms he swayed
He hath bidden his broad deep dromonds in readiness to be made;
Pinnaces, barges, and galleys and war-ships all are arrayed.
By Alexandria's city where the long wharves meet the tide
Made ready for the sailing doth all his navy ride.
At the entering-in of the summer, in the garland-days of May,
The Emir brought a-shipboard his countless war-array.
Now shake they forth the canvas, now is the voyage begun,
Nor shall the fair wind fail them till the shores of Spain be won.

192

Huge was the host of the heathen; the ships fast over the flood
Sailed like sea-monsters swimming and guiding themselves as they would.
From the height of the masts and the yard-arms great lamps like rubies swung;
From aloft such ruddy splendour over the waters they flung,
That across the sea their pathway was paved with a glory-flame;
And when at the last to the waters of the land of Spain they came,
With brightness as of the dawning lit up was the country-side.
Straight tidings came to Marsila of the help from afar descried.

193

The host of the heathen rein not their speed as onward they sweep;
They fleet over sheltered waters, they have passed from the outsea-deep;
They have left Marbrise to windward, on the lee Marbrose sinks low;
Now rides that proud armada on Ebro's deep swift flow.
Through the night from mast and yard-arm great lamps like rubies swung,
And afar their ruddy splendour o'er the darkling land was flung;
And they came unto Saragossa while yet the day was young.

194

Fair is the morn, bright shineth the sun: from the deck to the strand
Leaps the Emir; Espanliz the mighty at his right hand
Goeth, and follow after seven and ten proud kings,
With noble counts and war-dukes whose tale no minstrel sings.
'Neath a laurel amidst of a meadow a white silk pall men lay,
And thereon a throne fair-carven of ivory set they.
There Baligant, lord of the paynims, as a king is seated alone,
And around stand all those captains; and thus doth he speak from his throne:
"Give ear unto me, ye champions dauntless-hearted and free:
Long time have ye been of my good-will well entreated of me.
Henceforth this Charles, whom the Frank-folk name King and Overlord,
So much as to eat shall dare not, except as I give the word.
Long warring hath he wasted my Spain from strand to strand;
But now will I go and seek him in France his own dear land.

Long as my life endureth, I will not hold mine hand,
Until he be dead, or is kneeling in lowly submission to me."
As he spake, with his right hand's gauntlet he smote upon his knee.

195

So hath he spoken, and steadfast his mind is; he will not refrain,
For all the gold under heaven, from his purpose of marching from Spain
Unto Aix, where the great courts-royal of Charles be held alway.
Shout all his vassals consenting to the word their lord doth say.
Upon two of his knights he calleth, Clarien and Clarifan hight:
"Ye be sons of King Maltraien, who took evermore his delight
In fulfilling my commandments: lo, now I bid you fare
To Marsila in Saragossa; unto him this message bear:—
Now am I come to help him against his Frankish foes:
Wheresoever I meet them, in mighty battle with these will I close.
This gauntlet gold-embroidered shall ye give into his right hand,
And withal this staff all-golden, in token that I command
That he come and render homage to me as his overlord
Ere I into France march forward and smite this Charles with the sword.
And except he crave my mercy, and kneel at my feet, and forswear
The God of the faith of the Christians, the crown from his head will I tear."
"Sire, nobly hast thou spoken!" cried all those paynims there.

196

Spake Baligant: "Ride hence, barons: thou, bearing the gauntlet ride,
And thou the staff." "Dear master, so will we do," they replied.
Fast rode they on unresting till in Saragossa they stood.
Ten gates have they passed, on bridges four have they crossed the flood:
All streets were thronged with burghers gazing as these rode by.
But when to the Upper City the messengers drew nigh,
By the palace they heard an exceeding great and bitter cry;
For in thousands there were the paynims; with weeping and wailing wild
They lamented, their gods Mahomet and Tervagant they reviled,
And Apollo, of whom they had gotten no help in the evil day.
"Woe for us! What shall betide us?" each unto other 'gan say.

"We be whelmed in confusion and ruin; we have lost Marsila our lord,
For the hand of the King is smitten from the wrist by Roland's sword;
And Jorfaleu the bright-haired, we shall look on his face no more;
And Charlemagne shall conquer all Spain from shore to shore!"
—Lo, now are dismounting the envoys at the steps of the palace-door.

197

Beneath the shade of an olive to earth the messengers spring:
Two Saracens lead their palfreys thence to the stalls of the King;
Then each grasped other's mantle, and side by side fared on
Till the topmost floor of the palace those envoys twain had won.
They enter the vaulted chamber, and with one voice they cry
Their godless salutation in token of amity:
"Mahomet who hath our homage, and Tervagant our Lord,
And Apollo, O King, preserve thee, and the Queen may they watch and ward!"
But Bramimunde cried: "In folly exceeding to these have ye prayed;
For our Gods have proved them traitors, who rendered us little aid
At Roncesval, but suffered our good knights there to be slain:
Yea, and my Lord in the battle trusted them all in vain,
For his right arm there was smitten from his side; it is lost for aye,
By the sword of Roland the mighty, the Frank Count, shorn away.
Now under the dominion of Charles shall all Spain lie!
Ah me, what doom shall betide me?—O wretched, wretched I!
Alas that I have not a dagger, on the point thereof to die!"

198

Made answer Clarien: "Lady, speak not thus hopelessly.
Messengers from the paynim Baligant are we:
He saith, your King Marsila now will he help and defend.
Lo here his staff and his gauntlet by us unto him doth he send.
Four thousand ships to the Ebro have brought his host of war;
Pinnaces there and barges, and swift-winged galleys there are;
There stately dromonds be riding past all numbering.
A mighty man of substance and puissant is our King.
In France is he steadfastly purposed to seek this Charlemagne,

And there shall he cringe for mercy low at his feet, or be slain."
Spake Bramimunde: "Small profit of his purposed march shall he gain!
And all too near shall he find them, our Frank foes, even in Spain.
For seven long years have they tarried in the heart of this our land;
And their Emperor is a hero, a warrior mighty of hand:
Ay, liever would he perish in battle than turn him to flight.
Unto him no king under heaven is more than a child in might.
No man living he feareth, that he should not face him in fight."

199

But now spake King Marsila: "Let all such mistrust be!
My lords"—and he turned to the envoys—"unto me alone speak ye.
Ye see that to death I am wounded: I am heirless of daughter or son:
Slain yester-even in battle was one—mine only one!
Pray ye my Lord that he hasten to avenge my cause and me.
O'er the land of Spain your Emir hath right of seignory:
Freely to him I yield it, if he will have it so;
Only let him defend it against this Frankish foe.
Good counsel withal can I give him as touching Charlemagne,
And so shall your Lord subdue him ere the month to its end shall wane.
The keys of Saragossa shall ye bear to my suzerain,
And say, Charles cannot escape him, if he will but hearken my word."
Unto him the messengers answered: "Well hast thou spoken, Lord."

200

Then spake Marsila: "My vassals hath Charles the Emperor slain,
Hath laid in ruins my cities, hath ravaged my land of Spain.
On the banks of Ebro gathered now is his whole array;
Yea, from this city he lieth but seven leagues away.
Tell ye the Emir: 'Hither lead on thine host forthright!'
Then on his foe to-morrow ere eventide shall he light.
But of this do ye warn him also, that he come as looking to fight;
For they will not flinch from his challenge, these Frank lords unafraid."
The keys of Saragossa then in their hands he laid.
Thereat unto him in obeisance bent those messengers twain,
And they took their farewell, and turned them to seek their lord again.

So the envoys twain of the Emir in haste their steeds bestrode,
And forth of the gates of the city with eager speed they rode;
But they seemed, when they came to their liege-lord, men smitten with strange dismay.
Now the keys of Saragossa before his feet they lay.
Spake Baligant: "What hath befallen? Where now is Marsila the King,
Whom I bade come into my presence?" Spake Clarien answering:
"He is wounded—to death is he wounded. The Emperor yesterday
Was far in the mountain-passes, being fain to return straightway
Unto France, and he left a rear-guard, that his honour might take no stain:
And with these did Roland his nephew and Oliver remain,
And the Peers, and twice ten thousand Frank warriors armour-dight:
And the hero-king Marsila fell upon these in fight.
And the King with this Count Roland clashed in the battle-rout;
But so fiercely the Lord of the Marches with Durendal struck out,
That the right arm of Marsila from his body was wholly shred;
And his son, his well-belovèd, is numbered with the dead,
And all those vassal-barons whom the King to battle led.
So he fled, for he could no longer abide that combat's stress,
And vengeance-athirst hard after his flight did the Emperor press.
Now therefore the King requesteth that thou be his help and his shield,
And freely to thee the dominion of the land of Spain will he yield."
But when Baligant heard those tidings, he was sunken deep in thought:
For wilderment and sorrow well-nigh was he distraught.

"Not all hath been told, Lord Emir," again did Clarien say,
"As touching that great battle at Roncesval yesterday:
There slain was this Count Roland and his friend Count Oliver,
And all the Twelve Companions whom Charles hath held so dear,
And all that twenty thousand of the Frankish rearguard-host,
Albeit King Marsila his right hand there hath lost,
And the Emperor hotly riding hath pursued him fast and far,
And in all this land remaineth nor knight nor man of war:

On the stricken field all slaughtered or in Ebro drowned they are.
Encamped on the bank of the river even now doth the Frank host lie;
Yea, still in the land they linger within thy reach, full nigh:
If thou wilt, their home-returning shall be one long agony."
Then Baligant's face was lightened, his look was proud and high;
His heart waxed lightsome and joyous; he rose from his throne straightway,
And he cried to his waiting vassals: "Lords, make ye no delay:
Out of the ships leap shoreward. To horse! Ride fast to the fray!
If Charlemagne the agèd flee not in disarray,
Right well shall King Marsila be avenged this day, I trow;
In exchange for his right hand severed will I give him the head of his foe!"

203

The paynims of Arabia leap from deck to shore,
There were some who mounted horses, and some that strong mules bore:
At their lord's behest on rode they—should they do or less or more?
The Emir, at whose commandment that great host onward pressed,
Called to his side Gemalfin, the friend of all loved best:
"Lo, I command thee, order all my battle thou."
Upon his great bay war-horse the Emir is mounted now;
Four war-dukes ride beside him unto Saragossa-town,
And there at the steps of marble from the saddle he lighteth down:
Four noble earls low bowed them at his stirrup, to hold the same.
He mounted the steps of the palace—lo, a sorrow-stricken dame,
Queen Bramimunde, forth hasting to meet the deliverer came:
"Ah, gentle knight, I am widowed of my lord and King!" she saith:
"King Charlemagne's nephew hath ruined his glory, hath dealt to him death!"
And she fell at his feet; but the Emir gently upraised her again.
So into that chamber of sorrow sorrowing passed these twain.

204

Soon as the King Marsila beheld the Emir nigh,
Unto two Saracen nobles of Spain did the stricken cry:
"Now in your arms uplift me, to sit upright for a space."
In his left hand one of his gauntlets did the sorely maimed upraise;

Then faintly spake Marsila: "My Lord and King, Emir,
Herewith into thine hands freely all Spain I render here,
With my city and all the lordships thereto that appertain.
For me, I am utterly ruined, I and my people of Spain."
"In thine affliction afflicted am I too," answered he;
"Yet now I may not linger long time communing with thee,
For, well I wot, my coming this Charles will not abide.
Howbeit, I take this gauntlet and the pledge thus ratified."
From the dying King he turned him, and for sorrow and pity he wept:
Then down those stairs of marble to the palace-court he stept:
He gat him to horse; hard spurring he rode to his host straightway
So fast, that he came the foremost before that long array;
And, still as he rode, he shouted in folly of arrogance:
"On, paynims, on!—they be fleeing, these craven men of France!"

205

At dawn, when the first clear brightness of day through the darkness broke,
From his vision-troubled slumber Charles the Emperor woke.
Then Gabriel the Angel, whom God had sent to ward
His sleep, with hand uplifted made the sign of the Peace of the Lord.
The King to his feet hath risen, he layeth his armour aside,
And the good knights all unarmed them throughout that war-host wide.
Then sprang they upon their horses, and in eager haste rode they
By many a track far-stretching, by many a broad highway,
Being fain to look on the havoc, the strange wild ruin wrought
At Roncesval, where the battle, the Sorrow of France, was fought.

206

Unto Roncesval the white-haired King is come again;
And he brake forth into weeping when he looked upon all those slain.
Then he spake to the Franks: "Lords barons, go softly ye for a space,
For I needs must pass before you alone, till I look on the face
Of my sister's son, where Roland shall be found in the promised place.
For I mind me, at Aix at a yearly feast, how gallant knights
Vaunted of hard-fought battles, boasted of hard-won fights;

And thus cried Roland: 'Never in a strange land would I die,
Except afront of my vassals and my peers at the end I lie:
Unto the land of the foemen shall my face be turned at the last,
So to my rest like a hero, like a conqueror, I shall have passed.'"
Then, farther than a strong man his staff through air might fling,
Paced on before his barons and climbed a knoll the King.

207

As fared the Emperor seeking where might his nephew be found,
He beheld much grass in the meadow, flowers thickly bestarred the ground;
But all with the blood of our barons were wet, were crimsoned deep.
So stirred was he with compassion that he could not choose but weep.
He passed, at the top of the barrow, beneath a pine-tree's shade:
There, into the stones deep-bitten, were the strokes of Roland's blade.
There, on the green grass lying, his nephew's corse he beheld:
No marvel that Charles's anger as a stormy sea-tide swelled!
He leapt from the saddle, with hurried step to his side he sped:
He knelt, he enfolded in clasping arms the belovèd head;
Then, in anguish of spirit swooning, he sank down over the dead.

208

From his swoon the Emperor wakened; then nigh him Duke Naimes drew,
Count Acelin, Count Thierry, and Geoffrey the lord of Anjou.
They uplifted their King, they set him 'neath the pine that crowned that hill,
And he looked on the ground, and his nephew he saw, as he lay so still,
And he brake into lamentation, tenderly, lovingly:
"Ah Roland well-belovèd, may God have mercy on thee!
No man on the earth hath ever beheld so peerless a knight
To set in order the battle, to face the storm of fight.
Ah me! my royal honour henceforth shall sink and wane!"
And by anguish overmastered King Charles hath swooned yet again

209

Yet again the King reviveth from his swoon, and barons four
Bear him up in their hands: he looketh on the face of the dead once more,

On the body so goodly-shapen, on the bloodless visage wan,
On the eyes death-overshadowed, whence the glory of life is gone;
And in loyal love lamented Charles as he gazed thereon:
"Roland my well-belovèd, God raise thy soul to the skies,
To a place with the saints in glory mid the flowers of Paradise!
Alas for thee, knight and hero, that ever thou camest to Spain!
Never shall day pass over, but I mourn thee in heart-sick pain.
How shall my might and my glory into nothingness decay!
I have none to uphold mine honour now in the evil day!
Under the arch of heaven no friend is left to me now!
Kinsmen have I, but among them is no such hero as thou."
His hair with his hands he teareth: Franks round him in bitter grief
A hundred thousand are weeping in ruth for that lost chief.

210

"Roland my well-belovèd, unto France ere long must I fare;
And when I shall come unto Laon, to the halls of my palace there,
Strange men from many a kingdom will come and will ask of me,
'Where is the great war-captain?' I must needs say, 'Dead lieth he
In Spain!' I shall rule my kingdom in heaviness of soul:
No day shall dawn, but remembrance shall waken with weeping and dole.

211

Roland my well-belovèd, young hero comely and tall,
When again in Aix I am standing, in the hallowed minster-hall,
There will come to me men full many, will ask for tidings of thee;
And tidings shall I tell them of strange calamity:
'Dead!—dead is he, my nephew of the ever-victorious hand!'
And the nations will rise against me, the men of Saxon land,
Hungarians and Bulgarians, and heathens fierce and fell,
Apulian folk and Roman, and they that in Sicily dwell,
And the swarthy tribes of Afric, and the Moors of Califerne;
So daily my trouble and anguish as a spreading fire shall burn.
Then, who shall order the battle for me with such puissance,
When he is dead who captained ever the hosts of France?

O France, sweet France, of thy dearest thou sittest bereaved, forlorn!
So grievous is mine affliction, I would I had never been born!"
In his exceeding anguish his snowy beard hath he torn:
With both his hands is he plucking the silver locks from his head,
And Franks a hundred thousand lie swooning on earth as dead.

212

"Roland my well-belovèd, alas for thy life's short day!
May thy soul abide in the mansions of Paradise for aye!
Unto France exceeding dishonour the caitiff who slew thee hath done!
So deep is mine heart-anguish that I fain would no more live on;
For he died for me, and the dearest of all mine house is gone!
Unto God I put up my petition, to the Blessèd Mary's Son,
That, or ever unto the mountain-gates of Sizra I come,
My soul from my weary body may fleet unto its long home,
And may join the souls of my loved ones, and abide with my dearest and best,
And that where their bodies be buried my bones may be laid to rest."
And again he brake into weeping, and his snow-white beard he tore;
And cried Duke Naimes: "The sorrow of Charles is passing sore!"

213

Came the lord of Anjou, Count Geoffrey: "Sir Emperor," spake that knight,
"Let not thy sorrow, I pray thee, overpass what is meet and right.
Command that throughout this stricken field our slain be sought,
Whose death in this sore battle the men of Spain have wrought.
To the house of the dead command thou that the bodies of these be borne."
"It is well," the Emperor answered: "unto that end sound thine horn."

214

The voice of the horn of Geoffrey far over the war-host rang;
And the Franks, to fulfil the commandment of Charles, from the saddle sprang,
And they bare those friends and kinsmen, for the honour of France who had bled,
To a deep wide fosse delved ready, the silent house of the dead.
From the ranks stepped bishops and abbots, good clerks and canons came,
And tonsured monks, to assoil them, and bless them in Heaven's name.

And the orient myrrh they kindled, the incense-clouds upsoared,
With fervour of love upwafting their souls unto their Lord.
So, with all honour and worship, the earth hath covered them o'er;
And they left them alone with their glory—alas, they could do no more!

215

But the Emperor touching the body of Roland gave his behest,
And for Oliver and for Turpin, to keep them apart from the rest.
In his presence the doors they opened of life's most secret hall,
And they took forth the hearts of the heroes, and wrapped them in silken pall,
And under the dark-green pine-tree a several fosse they made;
There in white marble coffins those gallant hearts they laid.
Soft deer-skins round those bodies in fold over fold did they coil,
When first with wine they had laved them, and anointed with odorous oil.
Unto Gebuin and Tedbald then gave the King command,
And to Milo, and Otto the warder of the marches of his land:
"On three wains bear these homeward by pass and broad highway."
And with palls of the silk of Glaza those wains did they overlay.

216

Now Charles from the place of slaughter was even at point to be gone,
When from afar the coming of the paynim vanguard shone.
And forth three heralds spurring came from that great array
Bearing the Emir's challenge of battle, and thus did they say:
"Proud King, it nowise beseemeth that thou into France turn back:
Lo, Baligant the Emir fast rideth on thy track.
Exceeding huge is the war-host that he leadeth from Araby.
Now shall we see what valour is in this thy chivalry."
Then Charles the King in anger plucked at his beard of snow,
As rose to his remembrance the havoc and the woe
Which befell in that sore battle at Roncesval unto France.
Then upon all his war-host he looked with proud stern glance:
Far over the deep battalions his mighty voice rang clear:
"To horse, Frank knights and barons! Gird on your battle-gear!"

217

First of them all then armed him the Emperor in haste:
He arrayed him in his hauberk, his helm on his head he laced:
To his side he girded Joyeuse, the glorious sunbright brand,
And the shield in the Southland fashioned he slung from the broad neck-band;
And the spear that he grasped made lightnings as the point through the air he swung;
And now on his mighty war-horse Tencendour hath he sprung.
That steed had he won in battle at the ford below Marsonne,
When dead he hurled from the saddle Malpalin of Narbonne.
Once and again he spurred him, he cast on his neck the rein,
And afront of thirty thousand warriors rode amain,
And he cried unto God to help us, and the holy Apostle of Rome—
No fear, after that petition, had he to be overcome!
And the Franks cried: "Lo, a hero mighty in war-renown!
Such should a king be ever who would worthily wear a crown!"

218

The warriors of France are leaping from the saddle the wide field o'er;
They are girding on their harness, a hundred thousand and more.
Clad all in glittering armour, war-hardened fighters they showed;
Full knightly were their weapons, and fleet the steeds they rode;
The banners above the helmets flutter and stream out wide.
In saddle now are they settled, and like proven knights they ride:
Hot-hearted they are for the onset so soon as they meet their foes.
Charles looks on the goodly faces where the light of battle glows,
And unto his side he calleth Joseran lord of Provence,
And Naimes the grim grey war-duke, and Antelme of Mayence:
"A man in such true vassals may verily trust unto death!
A fool should he be whose courage amidst these faltereth!
Except yon Arab paynims repent them ere they draw near,
For the death of the good knight Roland soon shall they pay right dear!"
"Now God fulfil our petition!" spake Naimes the noble peer.

219

Then Charles called unto him Rabel and Guineman the tried and true,
And spake the King: "Lords barons, this is mine hest unto you—
Unto me in the place of Roland and of Oliver be ye now:
Sword Durendal thou bearest, and the great Horn Olifant thou.
So shall ye ride in the vanguard, with thousands five and ten,
Young knights of France, around you, all chosen valiant men.
Next these, in our second battle, shall be even as many as they,
And the lords Loranz and Gibuin shall lead them to the fray.
And Naimes the wise old war-duke and Count Joseran this day
Shall be over all, for the ranging of the host in battle-array.
There shall be, when they meet the foemen, a great and gallant fight,
Ay, knightly blows with the war-glaives, the scythes of death, will they smite."

220

All Franks be they of the foremost and the second battle-band:
Behind, in the third of the squadrons, Bavaria's vassals stand:
There good knights twenty thousand in mailèd hauberks flash—
Not they shall be slack in the battle when the fronts of onset clash!
Of all folk under heaven dearer to Charles are none
Save the Franks, whose conquering banners through all the world have gone.
And the Count Ogier of Denmark, a mighty battle-lord,
Shall lead them where heroes be reaping the harvest of the sword.

221

Lo, now hath Charles three squadrons ranged, and the fourth is arrayed
By Naimes the Duke, all barons of great hearts undismayed.
These be Germania's Markmen; thousands twice ten be they,
As the minstrels sing who have chanted the glory of that day.
Right goodly are their horses, and their weapons keen and bright.
Ay, liever will they perish than flinch from the sternest fight.
Hermann the Lord of Thracia captained that company:
He will not be a battle-blencher, far gladlier would he die!

222

Naimes the Duke and the good Count Joseran set in array
The fifth of those great squadrons, and Norman men are they:
Of these there be twenty thousand, the Franks know well their tale;
Swift be their battle-horses, and bright their linkèd mail.
They will look upon death unquailing, they will never flinch from the fray;
There is no folk under heaven so stubborn in battle's day.
Richard the old war-captain shall lead them in fighting field;
His lance is the piercer of hauberks, the shatterer of the shield.

223

In the sixth of those great squadrons were men of the Breton land;
Of good knights thirty thousand was that stalwart warrior-band.
Like gallant barons they bare them as onward they swept to the fight
With spear-staves banner-girded, with lances borne upright,
With fair-emblazoned bucklers whose devices gleamed afar;
And Eudes was their war-lord, a vassal trusty in war.
Chief of their first battalion was the good Count Nevelon,
And Tedbald of Reims the second, and Otto the third led on.
And their Lord cried: "Lead my people: I confide their honour to you!"
And the three with one voice answered: "Thy bidding will we do."

224

So of his battle-squadrons six be arrayed for the King;
And the seventh the wise old war-duke Naimes is ordering.
Here men of Poitou be marshalled, and barons of Auvergne,
Good knights forty thousand, warriors fearless and stern:
Strong are their great war-horses, and bright is their hauberk-mail.
These 'neath a ridge of the mountain be marshalled in a vale.
His right hand Charles uplifted, and he blessed that host of the Lord.
Count Joseran and Godselm led these battleward.

225

Duke Naimes himself hath marshalled the eighth war-company,
And these be the Flemish barons and the Frisian sons of the sea,

Knights more than two-score thousand—no battle-blenchers they!
"These will do loyal service!" did the King rejoicing say.
Captains of these are Rembald and Hamon, Galicia's son,
To lead them on knighthood's pathway where glory shall be won.

226

Naimes and Count Joseran marshalled in long lines o'er the plain
The ninth of the squadrons, warriors whose valour knew no stain;
For these were the lords Burgundian and the warriors of Lorraine.
They were good knights fifty thousand—for their captains took the tale;
They had laced on their heads their helmets, they were sheathed in the linkèd mail.
Their swords to their sides be girded, shields swing from their necks, and sway
Their lances strong whose spear-shafts be short—close fighters they!
If the men of Arabia meet them, if they shrink not back from the fray,
But grapple with these, with crashing blows will their line sweep on.
And the captain of these is Thierry, the noble Duke of Argonne.

227

They of the tenth of the squadrons, knights of France they are;
And these be a hundred thousand of our mightiest men of war:
They have goodly frames, and faces where glows the battle's light,
Though many a head is silvered, and many a beard snow-white.
All these in strong-knit hauberks of double link be arrayed;
There be some with the French steel girded, and some with the Spanish blade.
Upon each knightly buckler fair blazonries shine clear,
And of tempest-toughened ashwood is the shaft of each keen spear.
Now have they mounted their horses, they shout for the onset-word:
"Montjoy!" they cry: amidst them is Charlemagne their Lord.
The lord of Anjou, Count Geoffrey, beareth the Oriflamme;
Once was it Saint Peter's banner, and Roman was its name,
But now, from the Sword thrice-hallowed, Montjoy have they called the same.

228

The Emperor dismounteth; on the green grass kneeling low,
He turneth his face to the sunrise, to the east and the morning-glow,

And in fervent adoration to God most high doth he pray:
"True Father, for my defender and shield draw near this day,
Who wast there in the horror of darkness where Jonah the prophet lay
In the body of that sea-monster through days all-sunless three;
Who didst hearken and spare when repented the king of Nineveh
With his city, when sixscore thousand in dust and ashes kneeled;
Who didst from that strange torment the head of Daniel shield,
When into the den of lions the man of prayer was cast;
In the burning fiery furnace with the Children Three who wast;
May thy love this day not fail me; have me and mine in ward:
For thy mercy's sake, if it please thee, this boon unto me accord,
To avenge my nephew Roland, who died for the Faith of the Lord."
Again to his feet uprising, when thus the King had prayed,
The sign of the Cross on his forehead, the sign of power, he made;
Then again on his fleet-foot war-horse mounted the King of France,
While held for him was the stirrup by Naimes and Joseranz.
And now his massy buckler and his keen lance graspeth he:
Goodly he is of body, and he beareth him gallantly;
Bright is his face and shining with the light of victory.
He sat like a rock his war-horse as he dashed across the field,
While to rearward and to vanward the war-horns' challenge pealed.
High over the blast of the others the voice of Olifant soared,
While wept the Franks for compassion of Roland its perished lord.

229

Onward the Emperor rideth, all grace and goodlihead;
Over the breast of his hauberk his silver beard hath he spread,
And for love of their lord so do they down that long battle-line:
There be Franks a hundred thousand; ye may know them by that sign.
They pass by the peaks of the mountains, by frowning cliff and scaur,
Through deep dark gorges and defiles where manifold perils are,
Till forth of the mountain-portals they come from the desert land,
And lo, upon the marches of the realm of Spain they stand.
In the midst of a plain they range them in ordered battle-array.
Unto Baligant the Emir his watchers hasten away,

8—2

And a Syrian rider telleth to his master all the thing:
"Lo, yonder Charlemagne cometh! We have seen that haughty King:
High-hearted be his vassals, they will fail not their lord in the fray:
Gird on your armour! Battle shall ye surely have this day."
Then Baligant cried: "Fair tidings be these for a brave man's ear!
Blow up the horns, that my paynims may know that battle is near."

230

Then far and wide through the war-host they bade the tambours cry:
Pealed clarions and trumpets and war-horns wild and high.
The paynims leap from the saddle, and their war-array they don,
And in eager haste the Emir girdeth his armour on.
He arrayeth him in a hauberk fair-decked with broidery-hem,
He hath laced on his head a helmet that flasheth with gold and gem;
Thereafter hath he girded his sword to his left side,
The brand for the which he had found him a name in his arrogant pride;
For he said, when he heard the story of Joyeuse the sword of the King:
"For mine own, 'Précieuse' will I call it; the name hath a triumph-ring."
That name he made his war-cry, by his knights in the fight to be cried.
By its belt from his neck was hanging his buckler long and wide:
A border of diamonds glittered round the boss of burnished gold,
And a rosy silken baldric did its massy weight uphold.
His spear in his grasp he swayeth, Maltet it hath for name;
Thick as a mace of oak-wood is the huge-wrought shaft of the same;
And the steel alone of the lance-head a mule's full burden should be.
Now Baligant on his war-horse is mounted gallantly—
Held by a prince was the stirrup, Marcule from oversea:—
He is goodly of form: lean-waisted he is as a hound of the chase,
Great-thighed, broad-flanked, deep-chested, his frame all sinewy grace:
Clear-eyed he is, broad-shouldered, with long and wavy hair,
Gallant of face—as a flower in summer, so is he fair.
Well proven hath been his valour in many a stubborn fight.
Ah God! had he been but a Christian, he had been a noble knight!
He spurs to the leap his charger, till the bright blood starts from its side:
Clear over a gully he bounded, fifty feet was it wide.

And the paynims shouted: "The marches safely and well shall he ward!
No Frank there is but shall tremble to joust against our Lord:
Will he or no, he shall forfeit his life, in dust laid low.
This Charles is a very madman that he fled not long ago!"

231

Like a very flower of knighthood doth the Emir onward ride;
White is his beard long-flowing, as a lily in April-tide;
All hidden lore of the holy heathen books he knows;
He is dauntless in the battle, a scorner of his foes.
At his side is his son Malprimès, a prince of knightly mood:
Tall is he and strong, for he shameth not his fathers' blood.
He cried to his sire: "My father, on let us ride apace,
For fain would I know if surely we shall look this Charles in the face."
And Baligant said: "That shall we, for he is a warrior bold:
In many a lay and record is the tale of his glory told.
But now hath he Roland his nephew no longer to aid him in fight,
And little his strength shall avail him, I wot, to withstand our might."

232

"My noble son Malprimès," Baligant spake again,
"Yesterday that good vassal Roland in fight was slain.
And Oliver, a knightly and passing-valiant peer,
Yea, all the Twelve Companions, whom Charlemagne held so dear;
And of twenty thousand warriors of France not a man doth live;
And for all that now be left him my glove would I not give.
O yea, the King returneth: my Syrian messenger
Saith that in ten huge squadrons his host was marshalled there,
Saith, that a mighty warrior doth the great horn Olifant bear,
And his fellow-captain soundeth a clarion pealing clear;
And they ride afront of the vanguard of that great war-array;
Franks fifteen thousand onward sweep after each to the fray:
Young knights be these whom 'his children' Charles is wont to name:
And behind them thousands as many press onward war-aflame.
Doubt not, hard blows shall be stricken by these full dauntlessly."
And Malprimès said: "In the battle the first stroke grant thou to me!"

233

And Baligant made answer: "Fair son Malprimès, to thee
Fain am I to grant whatsoever boon thou wouldst ask of me.
On then! against yon Frenchmen ride forthwith and smite!
Take with thee the King of Persia, Torleu, to ride on thy right,
And Clapamort the Wiltzian on thy left shall charge to the fight;
And if thou to the dust canst humble the pride of the arrogant,
Of the warrior chief who soundeth the great horn Olifant,
I will give of my land for guerdon a goodly portion to thee,
Even all that from Cheriant stretcheth down unto Val-Marchis."
And he answered: "Sire, I thank thee for the promised seignory."
Before him he bent, and the earnest thereof he received from his hand.
In the olden time King Fleury ruled that selfsame land.
Alas for his hope!—for never on that satrapy did he look:
Therewith was he never invested, nor possession thereof he took.

234

All down the lines of his war-host the Emir rideth on;
Followeth hard behind him the giant form of his son;
King Clapamort and King Torleu to smite at his side are gone.
Then in thrice ten huge squadrons they marshalled their array,
Horsemen riding on horses, a marvellous host were they:
There were warriors fifty thousand in the least of them all that day.
And of these, the men of the kingdom of Butenrot marched in the first—
The land of Judas, betrayer of God for the silver accurst;—
In the second were men of Misnia, huge-headed, backed like the boar,
For with horrent-ridging bristles behind were they covered o'er;
In the third were they that from Nubia and the land of Blos were sent;
In the fourth the Slavs and the Russland warriors battleward went;
The men of Sorz and Sorbia in the fifth of the squadrons stood;
In the sixth the men of Armenia and the swarthy Moorish brood;
In the seventh squadron marshalled was the host of Jericho;
The eighth was of negroes wholly, the ninth of the men of Gros;
In the tenth were the evil-hearted men of Balide-la-fort;

By the body and might of Mahomet their emir-captain swore:
" This Charles of France cometh riding like a madman frenzied-souled!
Fierce fight shall we have, if his courage ere this have waxed not cold,
And never his head hereafter shall wear its crown of gold."

235

    Then other ten great squadrons in battle-array he placed.
In the first were the Orcaneans, a people demon-faced,
Which had come from Val-fui marching over many a league of land;
In the second ranged be the Turkmans, in the third the Persians stand;
In the fourth be the fierce Chananeans, in the fifth be the men of Avère
And of Soltras; the sixth is of Euglès, and the Ormaloes be there;
In the seventh be the Samiel people, in the eighth be Borussia's swords;
In the ninth be the Slavs, and Occiant in the tenth hath her desert-hordes—
A people that worship never our Lord, nor to God do they pray:
Thou shalt never hear of paynims more evil-souled than they.
They be treacherous fighters and cruel, their skins as iron are hard,
Therefore they need not helmet nor hauberk their lives to ward.

236

    Yet again the Emir arrayeth squadrons ten of our foes.
In the first be sons of Anak, the giants of Malprose;
In the second be Huns; Hungarians in the third to battle ride;
In the fourth be the men of Baldisa, a land exceeding wide;
In the fifth of the squadrons marshalled be the men of Val-Peruse;
In the sixth be the ranks embattled of Aiglet and Marmuse;
There be warriors of Leus in the seventh, and the men of Astrimon;
In the eighth be the men of Argilla, in the ninth the men of Clarbonne;
In the tenth be the men of Val-Fonda, the bearded foes of the Lord.
So these be the thirty squadrons, as the annals of France record.
Most huge is the host, and the trumpets' blare goeth up to the skies
As onward ride these paynims in passing gallant wise.

237

    A lord of wide possessions is the Emir, a man of might.
Before him the Dragon-standard leadeth his host to the fight:

The ensign of Mahomet and of Tervagant goeth thereby;
And there is the false god's image, of Apollo, lifted high.
Thereby ten Chananeans rode upon either side,
Shouting the proclamation of prayer, and thus they cried:
"Whosoever craveth protection of these our Gods this day,
Let him now bend low in homage, and to these right humbly pray."
Then lowly bowed each paynim his head upon his breast:
Long lines of shining helmets were drooping the lofty crest.
And the Franks beheld it—"Caitiffs, ye shall die full soon!" they said:
"This day in confusion of havoc shall your host be discomfited.
Our God shall be shield and defender of Charles from your myriad hordes;
In His name now will we triumph, for the battle is the Lord's."

238

The Emir in all war-wisdom is cunning, a captain tried;
And now his son hath he summoned with those two kings to his side:
"Lords barons, ye in the onfall before mine host shall ride,
And all my battle-squadrons to victory shall ye guide:
But three of the best of the thirty with me shall here abide;
Let the first be the Turkish squadron, the second the Ormaloes,
And the third those sons of Anak, the giants of Malprose:
Yea, also the Occiant serried ranks round me shall close.
And with these will I clash in combat with Charles and his Frank array:
If the Emperor be so hardy as to face me in the fray,
Swept by my sword from his shoulders his head shall be forthright:
So is his sentence determined; he hath none other right!"

239

Huge are the hosts, and the ordered lines be a goodly sight.
Now 'twixt those fronts of battle is ridge nor vale nor height,
Nor forest nor copsewood hideth foeman from foeman's eyes:
They are clear to be seen, for an open plain betwixt them lies.
Then Baligant cried: "My paynims, on! Charge down on the foe!
With my banner before you doth Amboire of Oloferna go!"

Outpealed the paynim war-cry: "Précieuse! Précieuse!" they shout.
"This day," cried the Franks, "shall ye perish in havoc of ruinous rout!"
And once and again their war-cry "Montjoy! Montjoy!" rang out.
Then the Emperor bade sound trumpets, and a thousand war-horns roared;
But high o'er their shattering thunder the voice of Olifant soared.
And the paynims murmured: "The warriors of Charles be goodly to see!
This battle for us shall be stubborn, and stern shall the grapple be."

240

Wide is the level lowland, the great plain stretcheth afar;
Long be the fronts of battle, and deep the ranks of war.
Far flashed the burnished helmets where gold and gemstones shone,
And the bucklers and the mailcoats with the broidery thereon.
Gleamed many a swaying spear-head, waved many a gonfalon.
Blew up a thousand war-horns, their voices pealed out clear;
But high over all the roaring of Olifant might ye hear.
Then did the Emir summon his brother to draw near—
Canabeus hight that warrior, the King of Floridee,
Who hath that land in possession so far as Val-Sevree.
Toward those ten battle-squadrons of Charles he waved his hand:
"Lo there the pride and the glory of France the vaunted land!
See where mid his bearded barons doth the Emperor gallantly ride.
Over the breasts of their hauberks their beards be all spread wide,
Beards of old war-worn warriors, as frozen snow they are white.
Ha, with their swords and lances right hardily will they smite!
Now shall we clash in battle, a battle bitter and stern.
Never hath mortal witnessed such fury of war-flame burn!"
Then, farther than staff of a shepherd by a strong man's hand may be tossed,
Baligant rideth forward afront of his mighty host;
And rang his shout far-pealing adown that long array:
"On, paynims! myself before you will cleave the glory-way!"
As he spake it, his quivering spear-shaft on high his hand upbore,
And the steel thereof was pointed at Charles the Emperor.

241

When Charlemagne marked the Emir, and the Dragon-device that shone
On his banner, and all those myriads, as Arabia's host swept on
Over the lowland country, and covered all its face
Save where the Emperor's squadrons grimly held their place,
Then shouted the King of Frankland, and his voice pealed wide and far:
"Franks all, ye knights and barons, gallant vassals ye are,
In many a battle triumphant, victors in many a war!
Behold yon paynims—felons all and cowards they be,
And all their Law of Mahomet is worth not a denier-fee!
And though they be never so many, for that, lords, what care we?
Now, whoso would fain set forward, with me to the fight let him come!
For me, I will not refrain me or ever I charge them home."
The flanks of his mighty war-horse he touched with the gold of the spur,
And with four great leaps on bounded the good steed Tencendur.
"Our King is a hero!" shouted the Franks with one accord;
"Ride on, ye barons! No man this day shall fail our Lord!"

242

All cloudless was the morning, the sun in the heavens shone bright;
Huge were the squadrons ordered in long lines armour-dight:
Now are the rushing battalions at point to close in fight.
Then did the good Counts Rabel and Guineman charge amain,
As loose on the neck of the battle-steed they cast the rein,
And spurred on fast: from the charging Frenchmen pealed the cheers,
As the gallant lines swept onward couching the long keen spears.

243

A doughty knight is Rabel, his spurs of the fine gold sting
The flanks of his steed as he chargeth on Torleu the Persian King.
Against his lightning spear-point nor shield nor mail could hold:
Deep into the paynim's body plungeth the lance's gold:
Hurled down dead from the saddle mid the heather his corpse is rolled;
And the Franks beheld it, and shouted: "The stroke of God our aid!
For Charles and the Right! Let no man falter, no heart be afraid!"

244

Even then on the King of the Wiltzians swift death Guineman brought,
For his lance-head crashed through the buckler with flower-scrolls over-wrought:
Through the shattered links of the hauberk did that death-lightning leap,
Yea, and the very pennon in his body was buried deep.
Dead was he hurled from the saddle—let who will laugh or weep!
Then shouted the Franks acclaiming his war-triumphant might:
"Strike so, strike so, ye barons! Let none be slack to smite!
For Charles! The right is on our side, the wrong with the paynim folk!
God for our cause! Through His champion the voice of His justice spoke!"

245

The Prince Malprimès bestrideth a goodly steed snow-white:
His giant frame he hurleth into the thick of the fight:
With blow upon blow down-crashing onward he thundereth:
Corpse upon corpse is he casting down that long lane of death.
And Baligant saw it, and shouted to captain and knight and peer:
"Barons, your King hath entreated you well this many a year—
Look on my son where he goeth questing Charles their King,
And all those Franks and barons to the fight is he challenging!
Never for better vassal could the King his father pray!
Charge to his aid! Let your lances to my son's side clear your way!"
At the words of the King flashed forward the lines of charging spears:
Grim was the crash of their onset, and the mad fray burned more fierce;
Yea, wondrous stern and bitter hath waxed the battle-strain.
Such sight none witnessed aforetime, nor any shall witness again.

246

Exceeding huge be the armies, high-hearted the squadrons are,
And now are all their battalions locked in the grapple of war:
Frank and paynim are smiting marvellous blows amain.
Ah God! how many spear-shafts already be shivered in twain!
How many shields be shattered, and corslets piecemeal hewn!
On the earth were the corpses lying like reeds by a tempest strewn;

And the grass, whose green and tender veil that field o'erspread,
Was now with the blood all crimsoned of the dying and the dead.
Then cheering on his warriors again the Emir said:
"Strike hard, strike hard, ye barons! Down with the Christian brood!"
And wilder waxed the battle, a stormy sea of blood.
Never before nor after was seen such frenzy of fight.
Yea, nought shall bring an ending thereto save the darkness of night.

247

Rang out the voice of the Emir once more to his war-array:
"Strike hard, ye paynims! Therefore are ye hitherward come this day!
Wives will I give you, winsome and passing fair to see:
Fiefs will I give to the brave man, with lordship and seignory!"
And the paynims answered: "Our duty it is to strike for thee!"
Lo, shivered are all their lances at that first onset-clash,
And a hundred thousand war-glaives forth of the scabbards flash.
Hath ever such horror of havoc, such mad war-turmoil, been?
He might say, who alive came through it, that a battle indeed had he seen.

248

Then the mighty voice of the Frank-king cleft the war-din through:
"Ho, lords and barons, I love you, I put my trust in you!
Many and many a battle with me have ye fought and won:
Many a realm have ye conquered, and many a king overthrown.
Well ye deserve, I know it, rich guerdon at mine hands;
My very life do I owe you, much more fair lordships and lands.
For your sons, for your heirs, for your brothers, on these let your vengeance fall,
For the dear ones who died in the battle yestreen at Roncesval!
Against yon paynims, ye know it, the right is on our side."
"Yea, Sire, thou hast spoken truly!" those loyal Franks replied.
Twenty thousand warriors that challenge of Charles have heard,
And all with one voice crying pledge unto him their word
Never to fail nor forsake him for sorest strait nor for death.
None is there, but like a giant his lance he brandisheth;

And they hew and they thrust with the war-glaives, smiting evermore.
The battle is wondrous bitter, a travail passing sore.

249

Through the heart of the strife on-riding the baron Malprimès fought :
Mid the sons of France sore havoc his mighty arm hath wrought.
But Naimes the Duke hath marked him from afar with proud stern glance :
In the might of a hero charging he coucheth against him his lance.
Piercing his buckler's cover unswerving the point held on ;
Rending his hauberk-lappets to his heart the steel hath gone ;
Deep into his body plungeth the flame-bright gonfalon ;
Dead mid seven hundred comrades that paynim champion fell.
" Montjoy ! " the slayer shouted, " Hence to thy native hell ! "

250

Then at Naimes the Emir's brother, King Canabeus, spurred hard :
He flashed out his sword—the pommel thereof was diamond-bestarred :—
On the forepart of the helmet of the Duke did the sword-edge light,
And the half thereof was shattered, so starkly did he smite.
Five of the helmet-laces that steel asunder shred :
No whit availed the skull-cap to shield that good grey head ;
Through the hood's fine-woven link-mail to the very flesh it passed,
And therefrom was a red strip severed, and down on the earth was it cast.
In sooth 'twas a mighty sword-stroke, that the Duke was dazed for a space ;
And indeed had he fallen, but holpen he was by God of His grace.
To the neck of his steed he clingeth, as his wildered senses reel.
Had he had but time, that paynim, a second blow to deal,
Of a surety that noble vassal dead in the dust had been laid ;
But already Charles hath seen him, and already hath come to his aid.

251

Now in exceeding peril is Naimes the Duke, and in pain ;
And the foe in his triumph hasteth to smite him yet again ;
But Charles is there—" Thou caitiff, now shalt thou rue that blow ! "
And in all his might and his valiance he clasheth against the foe :

He hath shattered his shield, its fragments are dashed against his heart;
The neck-piece of his hauberk is torn by the steel apart;
Clear through the paynim's body a highway of death is cleft;
Dead in the dust hath he hurled him; empty the saddle is left.

252

Then did sharp pangs of sorrow the heart of Charlemagne rend,
When grievously wounded before him he saw that good grey friend,
Saw how from beneath his helmet the blood bright-crimson fell;
And the Emperor spake to the hero, and counselled him wisely and well:
"My fair lord Naimes, henceforward ride thou hard at my side.
Dead is the miscreant felon through whom thou hast well-nigh died:
One thrust of my lance, and straightway on the shaft impaled is he!"
And the Duke made answer: "My liege-lord, I have utter trust in thee!
If I live, my life's devotion shall speak my thanks for me!"
Then charge they shoulder to shoulder in love and in loyalty;
Charge brave Franks twenty thousand beside them to left and to right,
Each man of them all a hero, mighty to thrust and to smite.

253

This way and that way rideth the Emir athwart the field;
His massy lance keen-cleaving doth his brawny right hand wield,
And before his thunderbolt onset the good Count Guineman reeled;
For over his heart hath he shattered the plate of his shining shield;
Rent is the mail of his hauberk, the links are scattered wide,
And the overlaps of his corslet are torn from either side.
Hurled from the swift steed's saddle dead is he laid on the plain.
Then rushed the slayer on Gebuin and Loranz, and slew those twain;
And Richard the agèd, liege-lord of the Normans, hath he slain.
And the paynims beheld, and shouted: "Précieuse! Précieuse! good sword!
Strike hard, strike hard, ye barons! Our help and our shield is our Lord!"

254

How glorious showed they charging, the knights of Araby,
Of Occiant, of Argilla, and the Bascle chivalry!

Mightily swung they the lances, fierce was their onset-shock ;
Yet their war-waves dashed on the Frankish front but as waves on a rock.
Ever are warriors falling, falling on either side :
No respite is yet in the battle, though it draweth to eventide.
Woe for the gallant barons of France that fall so fast !
Ah me, they shall have more anguish ere the day be overpast !

255

    Arabs and Franks in the grapple of death like giants smite ;
Snapped are the shafts of lances, and the steel heads burnished bright.
Whoso had seen the bucklers to glittering fragments dashed,
Whoso had heard the hauberks as the sundering link-mail clashed,
Whoso had heard the war-glaives on the helmets ring death's knell,
Whoso had seen the heroes as from saddle fast they fell,
Had heard the moans of the dying, on the hard earth as they lay,
Ah, long should he have remembrance of the woe of a fearful day !
Well-nigh past man's endurance was the agony of that fray.
Now to his god Apollo the Emir cried aloud,
To Tervagant and to Mahomet wildly he prayed and vowed :—
"My Lords and my Gods, I have served you faithfully all my days ;
But now in your temples your statues of fine gold wrought will I raise,
If ye will but help me to vanquish Charlemagne in this fray !"
Then met him his friend, Gemalfin, with tidings of dismay :
"Sire Baligant, ill is thy fortune ! Behold, Malprimès is dead,
Lost unto thee !—and thy brother Canabeus is sped.
Two of the Frankish warriors the glory thereof have won,
And of those deeds one, meseemeth, their Emperor hath done ;
For giant-framed was the slayer, and bare him like high-born lord,
And white was his beard as the lily that springs from the April sward."
When he heard those heavy tidings, the Emir bowed his crest,
And his head 'neath the stroke of affliction sank upon his breast ;
So torn was his heart with sorrow that in sooth he was like to have died.
Then called he Jangleu, the captain from overseas, to his side.

256

And the Emir spake to the captain: "Jangleu, hither to me:
Thou art a warrior dauntless; war-wisdom abideth with thee.
I have followed thy counsel ever—how goeth the day in thy sight?
Say, shall the Frank or the Arab be victor in the fight?"
But heavy of cheer he answered: "A dead man, sire, art thou!
Nothing thy Gods shall avail thee, nor help in thy need, I trow.
This Charles is death-defiant, a passing valiant lord,
And never hath man seen nation so mighty to wield the sword.
Thou, rally thine Occiant barons, Turks, Enfrons, Araby's host,
And the Giants—and do and delay not the thing that needeth most."

257

Over the breast of his hauberk his beard hath the Emir thrown;
It is white as the flower of the hawthorn when the buds of May are blown:
Howsoever befall the issue, of all men shall he be known.
To his mouth he setteth a trumpet that pealeth loud and clear,
And he sendeth the blast high-ringing, that all the paynims hear.
Through all that field then rallied his people, and thronged to his aid:
Like asses the men of Occiant brayed, and as horses neighed,
And like curs and hounds did the warriors of Argilla yelp and bay.
They hurled themselves like madmen all on the Frank array;
They burst through their densest battalions, the long lines swayed and reeled:
Seven thousand at that first onslaught laid they dead on the field.

258

Never a battle-blencher was the Danish Count Ogier:
Never a better vassal clad him in warrior-gear.
When he saw how the Frankish squadrons by the breakers of battle were rent,
His voice through the storm to Thierry the Duke of Argonne he sent:
Count Joseran called he, and Geoffrey, the lord of Anjou, to his side;
And in haughty indignation unto Charlemagne he cried:
"Dost see how the paynim myriads are hewing thy warriors down?
Now God forbid that ever thine head should wear a crown,

If now thou be slack in avenging the havoc and the shame!"
From lips of King or captain no word of answer came,
But each set spurs to his war-horse, and cast on his neck the rein,
And, where thickest the foes were surging, charged they down amain.

259

Now right gallantly smiteth Charlemagne the King;
Loud do the blows of Ogier the Dane and of Duke Naimes ring;
And the lord of Anjou, Count Geoffrey, beareth the banner high;
But Ogier of all is the chiefest in the might of chivalry;
For he spurred his steed till the charger like storm-scourged billow leapt;
Down on the princely bearer of the Dragon-standard he swept,
And the lord Amboire hurled earthward is dead at the feet of the Dane.
Fallen is Baligant's ensign, its splendour hath stooped to the plain!
When the Emir beheld the standard of the Dragon overthrown,
And the banner of Mahomet defenceless left and alone,
Then to that unbeliever's soul was the truth made known
That with him was the wrong and the treason, and with Charlemagne the right,
And chill grew the hearts of the Arabs, and they faltered back from the fight.
To the Franks the Emperor's challenge rang through the battle's roar:
"Answer—for God's cause, barons, will ye strike on my side once more?"
And with one voice all they answered: "What need that thou ask this thing?
Accursèd be he who strikes not with his might for our Lord the King!"

260

Now is the long day waning; to eventide it turns,
Yet the flame of the swords of paynim and Frank through the fight still burns.
Ha, they be hero-captains that rally the war-hosts there!
They forget not the war-cries that kindle courage out of despair—
"Précieuse!" the shout of the Emir, "Précieuse!" far ringeth round:
"Montjoy! Montjoy!" Charles shouteth, the war-cry world-renowned.
By the lion-voice far-pealing doth each the other know—
Now in the heart of the battle at last foe faceth foe!
With lances couched they are charging—like thunderbolts meeting they clash;
On the rose-emblazoned targes the lightning spear-heads crash;

Shattered the shields are under the golden bosses wide;
Rent are the laps of the hauberk, torn from the warrior's side;
Yet the spear-head slid by the body, the flesh was yet untorn;
But snapped were the girths asunder, and the saddles were earthward borne.
So fell those kings from their chargers; in dust for a moment they lay,
But they leapt to their feet undaunted, and their battle-blades drew they.
Now have they closed in a grapple the which none sundereth:
There shall be but one end only—'tis a fight to the very death.

261

A valiant champion of champions is Charles of France the Fair;
But the Emir's soul is unshaken, nor doubt nor fear is there.
The swords flash bare from the scabbards, the flame of the steel leaps high;
Down on the ringing bucklers they rain blows mightily;
They cleave bull's hide and the twofold oak of stubborn grain;
The studs start forth of their settings, the bosses are shivered in twain.
They have dropped the shards of their bucklers, in the shieldless mail they fight
'Neath the hailing sword-strokes leapeth red fire from the helmets bright.
Now nought but death can end it, this battle of the strong,
Except one yield to other, and own himself in the wrong.

262

Cried the Emir: "Charles, bethink thee, and bow thy proud heart low
To crave of me forgiveness: my son, full well I know,
Hast thou slain, and all unjustly of my realm dost make demand:
Yet become my vassal; I render it thee in fief to thine hand;
And thou as my man shalt hold it from hence to the Morning-land."
But Charles made answer: "Deepest dishonour thou offerest me!
Nor peace nor love can I render to paynim such as thee.
But thou, the law receive thou by God from Heaven sent,
The Faith of Christ: I will hold thee dear, if so thou repent
And become the believing servant of the King Omnipotent."
But Baligant answered: "Thou speakest but vain and evil words!"
And again they closed in the battle, and smote with the keen-edged swords.

263

A warrior tried is the Emir, a man of giant might:
On the helmet ruddy-gleaming of Charlemagne doth he smite:
Over his head is it shattered, and lo, a deep cleft there,
And the edge of the steel hath bitten down to the roots of the hair:
Of the very flesh hath it taken a shred like the palm of a hand,
And bared be the very skull-bones by the bitter-biting brand.
Staggered the King, that well-nigh had he fallen to earth therefrom;
But God willed not that his servant be slain or overcome;
And his holy angel Gabriel to his side hath stooped his wing,
And he cried in a voice heart-thrilling: "Remember thy might, great King!"

264

When the voice of the holy Angel fell on the Emperor's ear,
No thought thenceforth of dying had he, nor any fear.
Suddenly woke remembrance and might, he saw all clear.
He smiteth the Emir's helmet with the sword—the Sword of France:
Crasheth the steel through the morion where gemstones gleam and glance:
It cleaveth the skull asunder, it dasheth abroad the brain,
And his visage down to his hoary beard hath it shorn in twain.
Dead to the earth hath he hurled him—dead beyond remedy!
Then, that his friends might know him, Charles shouted the rallying-cry
"Montjoy!" and thitherward hasted Duke Naimes as he caught that word.
He seizeth Tencendur's bridle, he mounteth the King his Lord.
Now turn and flee the paynims; God willeth that no more there
They abide: to the Franks is granted fulfilment of all their prayer.

265

The host of the paynims is fleeing, by the will of God our Lord!
Charles and the Franks follow after them fast with avenging sword.
"Now, lords," the Emperor shouted, "requite upon these your woes!
Pay vengeance' debt, accomplish your hearts' desire on your foes!
For they caused you to weep this morning; myself beheld your tears."
"Sire, we do well to be angry!" they shouted in triumph fierce.
With might and main with the sword-edge they hewed, and they thrust with the spears.
Few, few in the hour of vengeance escaped of all those fleers.

266

Dust-clouds through the heat roll upward as evening sinketh to night;
But still the paynims are fleeing, the Franks torment their flight.
So chase they through falling darkness till Saragossa is won;
And lo, a tower of the watchmen, and Queen Bramimunde thereon.
Around her canons many and clerks assembled were
Of the false faith God abhorreth ever: no man of them there
Was ordained of a holy bishop; untonsured was their hair.
And she saw that madding tumult and ruin of rout draw nigh;
And she hasted to King Marsila, and weeping did she cry:
"O noble King, our armies be wholly discomfited!
And the Emir—alas the dishonour!—hath fallen in fight: he is dead!"
When King Marsila heard it, he turned his face to the wall:
His head from the day he veileth, while tears of anguish fall.
Lo, he hath died of sorrow! So laden with sin is his soul,
That living devils bear it to everlasting dole.

267

Dead are the paynim thousands, save the remnant fleeing afar;
And Charles hath won this battle, is victor in all the war.
He cometh to Saragossa, her gate he battereth down:
He hears no warder's challenge, no man defends the town.
He taketh a city fenceless, his ranks through her highways sweep:
Victors on beds of the vanquished that night take rest in sleep.
Haughty is he in his triumph, the snowy-bearded King,
And to him hath Bramimunde yielded the city's tower-ring,
The lesser towers fifty, the sky-encountering ten.
Ha, when the Lord God helpeth, well worketh the toiler then!

268

Now is the day passed over, droppeth the veil of the night;
Clear shineth the moon, in star-land the lamps are flashing bright.
In the King's hand Saragossa lieth: forth doth he send
A thousand Franks through the city to search it from end to end.
The synagogues they enter and the mosques, whose every wall
With mallet and axe they shatter: they break in pieces small

The idols, till nought of falsehood remaineth or sorcery.
In God the King believeth, and vowed to His service is he.
The bishops have blessed the water of sprinkling; the heathen folk
In crowds to the font baptismal are driven, to take Christ's yoke
Upon them: if any gainsayeth the King's imperious word,
He commandeth, and straightway they hang him, or burn, or slay with the sword.
Thus out of heathen darkness have five-score thousand been
Redeemed, and be now true Christians, save only Marsila's queen.
To sweet France the King willeth that captive she be led,
And by cords of love drawn upward in the steps of Christ to tread.

269

Now hath the night passed over, unveiled is the day's fair face.
On the towers of Saragossa doth Charles his warders place:
Valiant knights a thousand must guard for the King her wall.
Now mounteth the Emperor, homeward to ride with his barons all,
And with Bramimunde, whom he leadeth in guise of a prisoner;
Yet is he minded that kindness only be shown unto her.
So in all joy and gladness that cavalcade rideth on.
In the victors' strength triumphant they pass beside Narbonne:
And so are they come unto Burdel, that city of renown.
There on Saint Sevrin's altar the Emperor layeth down
That great horn Olifant, brimful of costly gems and of gold—
That relic may pious pilgrims, who seek to it, yet behold.
On great ships there made ready the broad Gironde they passed;
And so unto Blaive is the body of Roland brought at last,
And Oliver his companion, the utter-stainless knight,
And Turpin the wise in council, the valorous in fight.
In coffins of white marble those lords of renown they lay
At Saint Romain; there lie they, those barons, to this day.
There did the Franks commend them to God and the Name Divine.
But onward by valley and mountain Charles rideth from that shrine;
For he will not rest till he cometh to Aix, nor slack his speed:
And at last on the steps of the palace he lighteth down from his steed.
Then straightway, when he hath entered the stately-builded hall,

He sendeth his heralds, the judges of his courts-royal to call.
Unto Saxony and Bavaria, Lorraine and Frisia-land,
Unto Almayne and Burgundia he sendeth his command,
To Poictevins, Normans, and Bretons, and to every wisest son
Of France—herewith beginneth the trial of Ganelon.

270

So fareth back in triumph the Emperor from Spain,
And to Aix, the goodliest city in France, he cometh again.
Up the steps of his palace he goeth, his hall hath he entered—there
Lo, Alda cometh to meet him, the lady peerless-fair!
"Where then is Roland the captain," unto the King she cried,
"Who plighted his troth at parting to take me for his bride?"
But Charles in exceeding dolour and heaviness standeth there;
Tears from his eyes are streaming, his hoary beard doth he tear:
"Sister and friend belovèd, thou askest tidings of me
Of a dead man!—yet right worthy exchange will I give unto thee,
Even the young Prince Louis; nobler in France is none.
He shall rule after me my dominions wide, for that he is my son."
"These words to me," answered Alda, "are meaningless and vain.
Now God and his saints and angels forbid that I remain
Alive on the earth, now Roland, my lord and my love, is slain!"
Pale groweth her cheek, she falleth at the feet of Charlemagne:—
Lo, she is dead! God's mercy upon that lady's soul!
And the barons of France for compassion mourned her, and wept for dole.

271

So to her end hath Alda the beautiful passed this day.
Howbeit the Emperor deemeth that she hath but swooned away;
And the King breaketh forth into weeping for pity of her pain:
His hand unto hers he stretcheth; to upraise her from earth is he fain;
But the lifted head on her shoulders heavily falleth again.
Now knoweth Charles of a surety that this indeed is death,
And unto her side four high-born ladies he summoneth.
To a nunnery they bear her, in the dim-lit chapel lay,

And there by her bier keep vigil till the breaking of the day.
They buried her hard by the altar like a queen in royal state,
And the King for her sake on the sisters bestowed lands goodly and great.

272

Unto Aix the royal city again is the Emperor come:
There, bound with chains of iron, Ganelon bideth his doom.
In the city before the palace he is, to a stake fast bound
By the varlets, and thongs of deer-skin are knotted his wrists around.
With staves they smite him, and scourge him with cords—no better fate
He deserveth! In bitter anguish for judgment so doth he wait.

273

In the ancient chronicle's record fair written doth it stand
How Charles sent forth his summons unto vassals of many a land
To gather in full assembly at Aix his chapel-hall:
And the set time was a high-day, a holy festival—
There be that affirm that the Saint's Day of Silvester the noble it was.
That day began the judgment and the trial of the cause
Of Ganelon, whose devising had that great treason wrought.
Now the Emperor giveth commandment that before him he be brought.

274

"Lords of the land and barons," King Charles said, "hearken ye!
This day judge righteous judgment 'twixt Ganelon and me.
He fared with me in mine army unto the land of Spain,
And by his contriving were Frenchmen twice ten thousand slain.
He hath reft from me my nephew, whom never more shall I see,
And Oliver the valiant, the flower of chivalry;
And the Twelve Peers also for lucre did he betray to their death."
Spake Ganelon: "Be I accursèd if aught I deny that he saith!
But this same Roland had wronged me as touching my gold and my land;
And for this I sought his destruction, for this his death I planned.
But for treason—I allow not that herein treason is!"
"Now take we heedful counsel," said the Franks, "as touching this."

275

Lo ye, in the Emperor's presence standeth Ganelon there:
His frame is goodly-shapen, his visage's favour is fair.
Had he been but a loyal vassal, he had seemed a noble knight.
He looked on the Franks, on the doomsmen appointed to judge the right,
On his thirty noble kinsmen who had gathered to his side:
With a great voice far-ringing unto them all he cried:
"For the love of God, ye barons, fair hearing to me accord!
I was indeed in the army of the Emperor my Lord,
And I served him at all seasons in love and in loyalty.
Howbeit his nephew Roland had a lodged hate unto me,
And to death did he adjudge me, to a death of shameful pain,
For through him was I forced to be herald unto King Marsila in Spain;
And, save by my wit and my wisdom, I had not escaped the snare.
For the doughty fighter Roland, I defied him then and there:
Yea, Oliver his comrade and the Twelve Peers I defied:
Herein must Charles and his barons bear witness on my side.
This therefore is private vengeance, but of treason not a whit."
"We will take heedful counsel," said the Franks, "as touching it."

276

Then Ganelon saw that his trial was even at point to begin.
Now at his side were there gathered thirty men of his kin;
And to one did the rest all hearken, for his masterful confidence;
Pinabel hight that baron, of the castle of Sorence.
The man was in speech full cunning to make the wrong seem right,
And withal a stalwart champion to maintain his cause in fight.
"O friend, unto thee I entrust me!" unto him Count Ganelon saith:
"Do thou this day redeem me from dishonour and from death!"
And Pinabel said: "A champion shalt thou have certainly.
No man of all these Frank-folk shall adjudge thee worthy to die;
But, if that the Emperor suffer that in lists of fight we meet,
My good sword so shall convince him that his own lie shall he eat!"
In lowly thankfulness bowed him Ganelon at his feet.

277

Bavarian barons and Saxon be now in council met:
On the seats of judgment are Normans and Franks and Poictevins set;
Allmans are these, and Teutons: but of all these was the mind
Of the men of Auvergne in judgment the most unto mercy inclined,
And to lend an ear ungrudging to the pleading of Pinabel.
Spake one to another: "To suffer the past to be past were well.
Let us then break off this trial, and make our prayer to our Lord
That to Ganelon for this trespass his pardon he accord:
Thereafter shall he serve him in love and in loyalty.
Lo, Roland is dead, and never his face again shall we see:
Never by gold nor by treasure may we bring him back from the grave,
It were folly that one should battle for the dead whom he cannot save."
None was there of all those barons but gave consent thereto,
Save only Thierry, brother of Geoffrey of Anjou.

278

Unto Charlemagne his barons returned, and they said to the King:
"Sire, we beseech thee to pardon Count Ganelon in this thing;
So shall he serve thee hereafter in love and in loyalty.
Let him live, we beseech thee; valiant and gently born is he.
Lo, Roland is dead, and never his face again shall we see;
Never by all earth's treasures may we bring him back from the dead."
"Unto me have ye all turned traitors!" the King in his hot wrath said.

279

When Charles was ware that his barons had failed him one and all,
For utter shame and sorrow did his head on the breast of him fall,
And he cried in passion of anguish: "Of mine honour am I stripped bare!"
—But lo, the knight Thierry before him standeth there:
Brother he is unto Geoffrey the noble Duke of Anjou.
Lithe is he in his body, sinewy, swarthy of hue:
His locks be dark as the raven, of stature is he tall,
Albeit in measure moulded, nor over great nor small.

With courtesy full knightly to the Emperor he spake:
"Fair lord, be thou not troubled so sorely for this thing's sake.
Thou knowest that well I have served thee—yea, in my forefathers' name
A place amidst these judges for myself might I rightfully claim.
Though the tale of Ganelon's wronging by Roland were never so true,
Yet to that loyal servant is the King's protection due.
This Ganelon is a felon! Betrayer of Roland he was;
And also to thee is he perjured, is traitor and foe to thy cause.
Therefore by doom of hanging do I adjudge him to die,
That his body be delivered unto pain's extremity,
As the due is of the felon who committeth felony.
And if kinsman or friend of the traitor take on him to give me the lie,
With this my sword which is girded now beside my thigh
To maintain my sentence and judgment ready here stand I."
"Meetly and well hast thou spoken!" did all the Frank lords cry.

280

Then in King Charles's presence forth did Pinabel stand.
Tall is he, stalwart and valiant, and swift of foot and hand.
Whomso he smiteth in battle but once, his life is sped!
"Thine is this cause, my liege-lord," unto the King he said:
"Give then commandment, I pray thee, that the tumult of voices cease.
Lo, Thierry hath given his judgment in presence of all these:
I say, in his throat he lieth!—and in combat this will I prove!"
Therewith in the Emperor's right hand he layeth his deer-skin glove.
"Sureties, whose lives on the issue shall hang," said the King, "I demand."
And for this did thirty kinsmen of Ganelon forth stand.
"And for these will I give surety[1]," again said the King our Lord.
And he bade that, biding the issue, all these should be kept in ward.

281

When Thierry was ware that the combat would not be denied nor stayed,
Straightway his right-hand gauntlet in the hand of Charles he laid.

---

[1] That, if their champion were victorious, Ganelon and they should be set free.

And the King by sureties pledged him by the combat's issue to stand.
Then in the lists four benches were set by the King's command:
There they whose lives depended on the combat's issue should sit.
Said the baron-deemsters: "Ordered is the trial as is most fit."
And he that ordered the matter was Ogier the warrior Dane.
Now for their steeds and their armour they call, those champions twain.

282

When these stand armed for the combat that pledged they are to achieve,
They confess them, and absolution and blessing they receive:
They hear the hallowing mass-chant, the sacrament they take,
And to holy house and cloister rich offerings they make.
Once more in Charlemagne's presence they stand; they buckle tight
Their spurs; they array them in hauberks shining and strong and light.
Upon their heads have they settled the helmets flashing afar;
And now to the sides of them girded the swords gold-hilted are.
From their necks the quartered bucklers are hung by the broad shield-band;
And they grip the long keen lances each in his strong right hand.
Then to the backs of their chargers lightly the champions leap,
And knights a hundred thousand could not choose but weep,
Out of their love for Roland, for the peril of Thierry the knight;
For God alone foreknoweth the issue of this fight.

283

Below Aix lieth a meadow that stretcheth wide and fair,
And the lists for the mortal combat of the barons twain be there.
Mighty men be the champions, and of courage all unstained,
And fleet of foot their chargers, and in battle-manage trained.
Now are the spurs deep-striking, on the neck loose lieth the rein,
Now clash they in the onset, they smite with might and main.
Crashed through the shields the lances, their plates asunder flew;
Rent were the links of the hauberks, the girths were snapped in two;
Borne backward over the cruppers to earth were the riders swept.
A hundred thousand warriors trembled thereat and wept.

284

Scarce have the two knights fallen ere again on their feet they stand;
Pinabel is right stalwart, lithe, swift of foot and hand;
Each rusheth to close with other—no war-steeds now have they—
And with great swords golden-hilted smiting hard they essay
To hew asunder the helmets: such giant blows they deal
That a marvel it is that unshattered abideth the morion's steel.
Thrilling with hope and with terror looked on each Frankish knight.
"Ah God," King Charlemagne murmured, "make manifest the right!"

285

Cried Pinabel: "Now, Thierry, take back thy words, and I
Will then unto thee do homage in love and loyalty;
Yea, I will hold my possessions of thee as my suzerain:
Only Ganelon's pardon of Charles the King do thou gain."
"Out on the thought! I loathe it!" fiercely did Thierry say:
"If I hearken to thee, a traitor may I be accounted for aye!
Let God decide between us! May He show the right this day!"

286

"Pinabel," crieth Thierry, "thou art full knightly-souled,
And tall thou art, and stalwart, and thy limbs be of goodly mould;
Thy peers all know thy valour—thou then from the fight refrain,
And thy peace and reconcilement will I make with Charlemagne;
And on Ganelon such vengeance shall righteous justice wreak,
That never shall day pass over but men thereof shall speak."
"Now God the Lord forbid it!" indignant Pinabel cried:
"Steadfastly aye am I purposed to stand by a kinsman's side!
Never will I be recreant for any mortal born!
Far gladlier would I perish than be such a thing of scorn!"
And again they swung up the war-glaives, again smote fast and hard,
Hailing blows on the helmets with gold and gems bestarred,
Till the sparks against the sunlight flashed in a fiery rain.
Henceforth shall there be no respite, no sundering of these twain:
There is but one end to the combat, that one or other be slain.

287

A passing valiant warrior is Pinabel lord of Sorence;
He smote on the helmet fashioned by the armourer of Provence;
Such flashes of fire sprang from it that the dry grass leapt into flame;
He thrust with the point of his war-glaive with sure and deadly aim;
He hath cleft Thierry's visor, that across his face it hung;
He hath gashed his cheek, that a fountain of blood therefrom hath sprung;
Rent is the hauberk from shoulder to waist by the sweep of his blade;
But Thierry from death was warded, for God himself was his aid.

288

Outflamed the wrath of Thierry when he felt that cruel gash,
When he saw the grass before him besprent with the crimson plash.
At his foe's helm ruddy-gleaming full starkly did he hew,
And the crashing blade to the nose-piece hath cloven it in two,
So that Pinabel's brains forth rushing on the head-piece spattered it round.
Once more the sword down lightened, and stretched him dead on the ground.
So with that last blow the victor he stood in the fight hard-fought;
And the Franks with one voice shouted: "A miracle God had wrought!
Now is it just and righteous that hanged be Ganelon,
And with him his sureties, his kinsmen, who staked their lives thereon."

289

So Thierry hath won that battle: lo, Charles to meet him doth stride
Swiftly, and four great barons come at the Emperor's side,
Duke Naimes, and Ogier of Denmark, and Geoffrey of Anjou,
And William of Blaye. His champion to his breast the Emperor drew;
With his cloak of the fur of the marten he wiped that face stained red,
And he cast it aside, and another o'er the Emperor's shoulders they spread.
With gentle and loving observance they stripped of his arms their knight:
On an Arab mule they set him, and with jubilant delight
Unto Aix they came, and dismounted the castle-court within.
And now beginneth the judgment of the traitor and his kin.

290

Now Counts and Dukes are summoned to the presence of their Lord:
"What think ye," he saith, "of the kinsmen whom I have kept in ward?
To plead the cause of the traitor Ganelon came they all,
And for Pinabel were they sureties, with him to stand or fall."
And the Franks with one voice answered: "Let there not live of them one!"
Then gave the King commandment to his headsman, the grim Barbrun:
"Go thou, hang all those traitors upon the accursèd tree!
And by this my beard and its hoary hairs I swear unto thee,
That thy life, if but one escape thee, for the life of him shall be."
"What task for mine hand were better than this?" did the man reply.
With a hundred serjeants he haled them to their doom all ruthlessly,
And on that tree evil-fruited did he hang them, knights thrice ten.
So is it—a traitor destroyeth with himself his fellow-men.

291

Thereafter Bavarians and Allmans homeward their steps all bent,
And Poictevins and Normans and Bretons; but, ere they went,
They decreed—and above all other for this did the Frank lords cry—
That by strangest, fearfullest torment Ganelon should die.
Then four great battle-horses to the midst of the field brought they;
To his feet and his hands they bound them, that outstretched in the midst he lay.
High-mettled and swift are the chargers, four serjeants lash them to speed
Unto where for each stands waiting a filly afar on the mead.
Ah, now is the traitor delivered to a death of hideous pain!
The joints of his limbs and his sinews on a living rack they strain,
Till suddenly all his body is to fearful fragments rent,
And with crimson streams down-rushing is all the grass besprent.
Ganelon dies as the traitor should die, as the dastard should die!
Shall a traitor live—to triumph, to boast of his felony?

292

So then when the Emperor's vengeance its righteous course had ta'en,
His bishops of France he summoned, of Bavaria, of Almayne;

And he said : " In my palace abideth a noble captive queen :
She hath hearkened to holy discourses, good works of faith hath she seen ;
She believeth in God our Saviour : baptism now doth she crave.
To the font, I pray you, lead her, that God her soul may save."
"Provide for her then godmothers," the bishops made reply ;
So the King assigned to her ladies of lineage proud and high.
At the Baths of Aix was gathered a vast and noble train
To behold at the font baptismal bowed low the Queen of Spain.
And a new name, Juliana, they found for the new-born dame
Who of her heart's conviction from death to the Christ-life came.

293

So is the Emperor's vengeance accomplished, appeased is his wrath,
And Bramimunde's feet have been guided to Christ along love's path.
The day hath waned to its ending, night veileth the land with shade,
And the King in his vaulted chamber his limbs to rest hath laid.
Lo, the Angel Gabriel cometh to him with the word of the Lord :
"Charles, summon thine Empire's armies, again must thou draw the sword !
Haste thou to the land of Bira, to help King Vivien
In Impha his city beleaguered by a host of paynim men ;
For the Christians for thee are crying, and God hath heard their prayer."
Sore loth was the Emperor thither on that far journey to fare !
"Ah, God," he crieth, "how burdened is my life with travail and pain !"
His hoary beard he teareth, from his eyes the hot tears rain.

This is the Lay of Turoldus, and this the closing strain.

For EU product safety concerns, contact us at Calle de José Abascal, 56–1°,
28003 Madrid, Spain or eugpsr@cambridge.org.

www.ingramcontent.com/pod-product-compliance
Ingram Content Group UK Ltd.
Pitfield, Milton Keynes, MK11 3LW, UK
UKHW010048140625
459647UK00012BB/1688